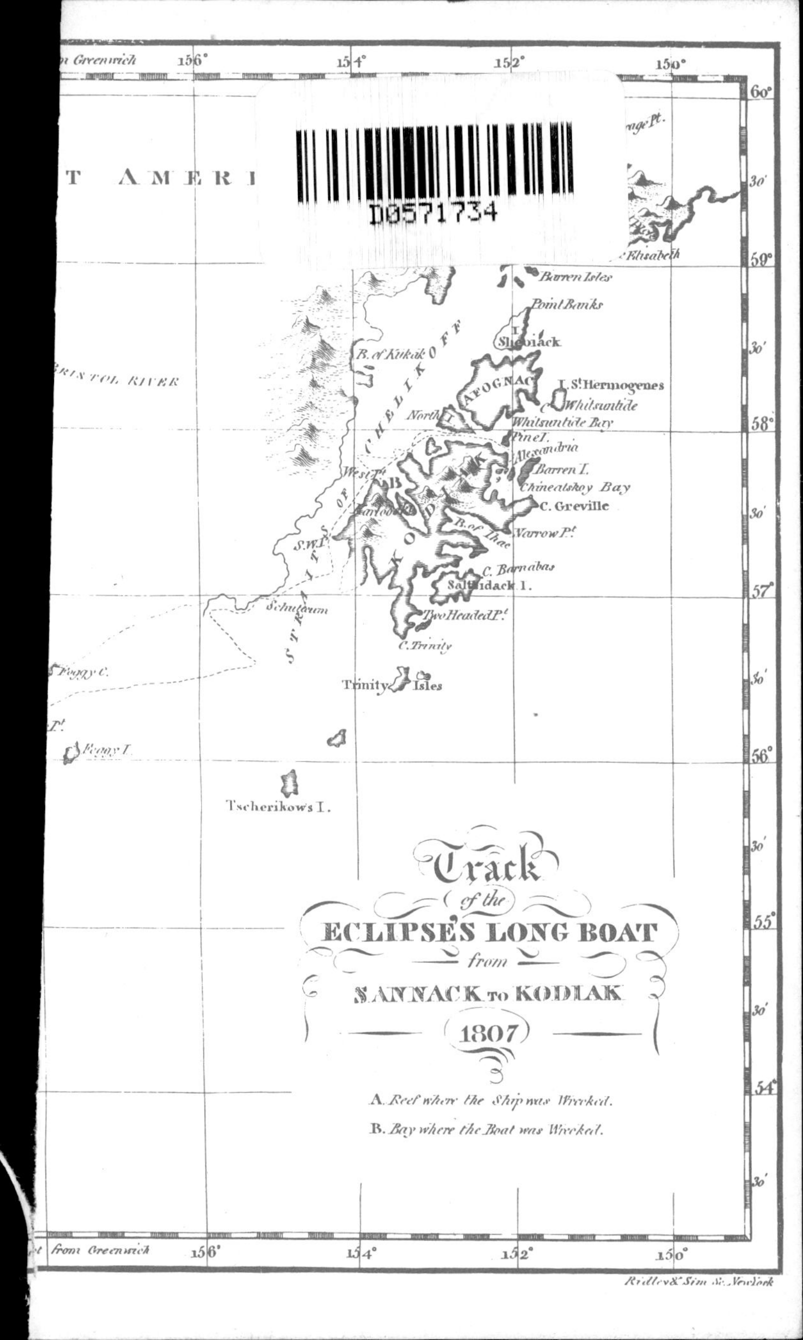

Greenwich
156°
154°
152°
150°
60°
30'
59°
58°
57°
56°
55°
54°
D0571734
T AMERI
Barren Isles
Point Banks
Shuiack
B. of Kukak
BRISTOL RIVER
STRAITS OF CHELIKOFF
AFOGNAC
I. St. Hermogenes
Whitsuntide
Whitsuntide Bay
North I.
Pine I.
Alexandria
Barren I.
Chinealskoy Bay
C. Greville
West Pt.
S.W. Pt.
KODIAK
B. of Ihac
Narrow Pt.
C. Barnabas
Salthidack I.
Schutarum
Two Headed Pt.
C. Trinity
Foggy C.
Trinity Isles
Foggy I.
Tscherikows I.
Track of the ECLIPSE'S LONG BOAT from SANNACK to KODIAK 1807
A. Reef where the Ship was Wrecked.
B. Bay where the Boat was Wrecked.
from Greenwich
Ridley & Sim Sc. New York

A VOYAGE ROUND THE WORLD,

FROM 1806 TO 1812;

IN WHICH

JAPAN, KAMSCHATKA, THE ALEUTIAN ISLANDS, AND THE SANDWICH ISLANDS WERE VISITED;

INCLUDING

A NARRATIVE OF THE AUTHOR'S SHIPWRECK ON THE ISLAND OF SANNACK, AND HIS SUBSEQUENT WRECK IN THE SHIP'S LONG-BOAT:

WITH AN ACCOUNT OF THE

PRESENT STATE OF THE SANDWICH ISLANDS,

AND

A VOCABULARY OF THEIR LANGUAGE.

BY ARCHIBALD CAMPBELL.

Facsimile Reproduction of the Third American Edition of 1822.

UNIVERSITY OF HAWAII PRESS
FOR FRIENDS OF THE LIBRARY OF HAWAII

HONOLULU, HAWAII, 1967.

MANUFACTURED IN THE UNITED STATES OF AMERICA

This edition is a facsimile reproduction of that originally printed by Duke & Browne of Charleston, S.C.

LIBRARY OF CONGRESS CATALOG CARD NO. 67-27051

Recommendation from his Excellency, the Governor of the State of New-York.

The second edition of a voyage round the world, by Archibald Campbell, has been recently published in New-York. The life of Campbell has been marked by extraordinary sufferings; and as there is no doubt of the authenticity of the work, I recommend it to the patronage of the public, from a persuasion that the merits and misfortunes of the narrator, entitle him to favorable consideration.

DE WITT CLINTON.

Albany, March 2d, 1820.

New-York, November 5th, 5819.

At a regular meeting of Morton Lodge, No. 108, (late No. 50,) held last evening, at their Lodge room, in the City of New-York, the following resolution was passed, viz.

"Resolved, that from the long acquaintance which we have had with brother Archibald Campbell, his regular deportment while sojourning with us, has induced this Lodge to recommend him, and they do recommend him to the kind protection and friendship of the fraternity generally."

Extract from the minutes.

S. W. ANDREWS, *Secretary.*
DANIEL SICKELS, W. M.
JOHN DEGEZ, P. M.

We, the undersigned, agree with the report of the officers of Morton Lodge, No. 108, (late No. 50,) with respect to the deportment of brother Archibald Campbell, and recommend him accordingly.

RICHARD O. PEARSALL, W. M. *Benevolent Lodge.*
JOSEPH FORRISTER, P. M. *Benevolent Lodge.*
JAMES S. TAYLOR, *Secretary Benevolent Lodge.*
ALEXANDER FRASER, *Treasurer Benevolent Lodge*
JAMES LYONS, Jun. P. M *St. John's No.* 9, *late No.* 6.
G. LANSING, P. M. *Phœnix Lodge No.* 40, *late No* 11.
JAMES WEBSTER, W M. *Abram's Lodge, No.* 83.
ROBERT YOUNG, P. M. *Abram's Lodge, No.* 83.
S. B. FLEMING, W. M. *St. John's, No.* 9, *late No.* 6

CERTIFICATE

By the Hon. Thomas H. Perkins.

Archibald Campbell, the author of a "Voyage round the World," made on board the ship Eclipse, in which I was interested, having applied to me to give him a certificate of the fact of his having been a seaman on board said ship, I readily do it.

His Book contains many interesting facts, and is worthy the perusal of persons who take pleasure in looking into works of this kind. His misfortunes, and the constant good deportment he has shewn since his return from the Sandwich Islands, give him a strong claim on the community.

T. H. PERKINS.

Boston, July 4, 1821.

*** The original documents are in the possession of the Author.

CONTENTS.

CHAPTER I.

Departure from England—Voyage to China—Transactions at Canton—Author enters on board an American ship—Passage to Kamschatka—Touches at Japan—Transactions there—Arrives at the harbour of St. Peter and St. Paul—Some account of the Russian settlement at that place. 15

CHAPTER II.

Departure from Kamschatka—Shipwrecked on a reef of rocks, on the northwest coast of America—Author with the rest of the crew, save themselves by the long boat—Are drifted on an island—Transactions upon the island—Prepare to build a vessel. 30

CHAPTER III.

Arrival of a party of Natives, and of the Russian Commandant of Oonalaska, who determines to send to Kodiak for assistance—Long-boat prepared for the voyage—Some account of Sannack or Halibut Island. 39

CHAPTER IV.

Sail from Sannack in the long-boat—Touch at the Island of Ungar—Distressing state of the settlement there—Sail from thence--Anchor at the village of Schutkum—Departure from it—Boat nearly embayed on the north coast of Kodiak--Arrived at Alexandria—Transactions there--Boat fitted out to return to Sannack. 47

CHAPTER V.

Departure from Alexandria—Boat forced into a bay by the weather, and hauled on shore--Obliged, by want of provisions, to leave the bay—A snow storm—The boat springs aleak--Is run on shore, and goes to pieces upon the rocks—A hut discovered, in which the crew pass the night. 58

CHAPTER VI.

A party quit the hut in search of a settlement--Author's feet frost-bitten—Progress of the party interrupted by a mountain—Return towards the hut, till prevented by the tide from passing a reef of rocks—Pass the night in a valley—Next morning set off at low water—Author falls behind, and in attempting to climb over a rock, gets his hands frost-bitten—Critical situation—Reaches the hut—Two Russians reach a settlement by the mountains, and send relief—Some account of Karlouski—Voyage to Alexandria. 63

CHAPTER VII.

Author carried to hospital—Both his feet amputated—Account of the party left at Sannack—Employed in teaching native children English—Account of Kodiak—Natives—Dress—Canoes—Superstition—Food—Author sails in the ship Neva for the Sandwich Islands. 71

CHAPTER VIII.

Voyage to Sandwich Islands--Make Owhyhee—Touch at Mowee—Proceed to Wahoo—Tamaahmaah and other chiefs come on board—Author resides three months with the King—Account of his mode of life—Remove to the house of Isaac Davis—Account of him—Death of Terremytee, the King's brother, and transactions that took place on that occasion—Remarkable water-spout—Author receives a grant of land from the King, to which he removes—Residence there—Arrival of the ship Duke of Portland—Anecdotes of the King—Departure from the Sandwich Islands. 85

CHAPTER IX.

Description of Wahoo—Extent—Whyteete-bay—Account of Tamaahmaah's navy—Town and harbour of Hanaroora--Bass's harbour—Wymumme, or Pearl-river—State of cultivation--Breed of cattle—Account of the white people resident on the island. 109

CHAPTER X.

Account of the natives—Personal appearance—Ranks--Power of the king—Priests—Capital punishments

—Mode of detecting theft—Religious belief—Places of worship and ceremonies—Macaheite—Houses—Food—Ava—Spirits distilled from the tee-root—State of the women—Marriages—Dress—Manufactures—Nets and lines—Modes of fishing—Trade—Price of provisions—Amusements—Funeral Rites—Military—Progress in civilization—Account of Tamaahmaah and family. 121

CHAPTER XI.

Departure from Wahoo—Pass Otaheite—Double Cape Horn—Arrival at Rio Janeiro—Transactions there, during a residence of nearly two years—Voyage home—and from thence to the United States. 157

APPENDIX No. I

A Vocabulary of the language of the Sandwich Islands. 165

APPENDIX No. II.

Statement of the Case of Archibald Campbell, by Dr. Nordgoorst, in the service of the Russian American Company. 189

APPENDIX No. III.

Notice of Archibald Campbell, from Blackwood's Magazine. 195

APPENDIX No. IV.

Historical Account of the Sandwich Islands. 203

APPENDIX No. V.

Notes. 211

PREFACE.

A PERUSAL of the voyages of discovery, which shed so much lustre on the reign of George III. naturally excites a strong desire to learn what effects have been produced among the nations whose existence they have introduced to our notice.

That the interests of science and commerce have been greatly promoted by these voyages, cannot be doubted; but it may be questioned whether the result has been equally beneficial to the natives of the newly discovered countries; and, as the editor* of Cook's last voyage justly remarks, "it would afford exquisite pleasure to every benevolent mind, to be instructed in facts which might enable us without hesitation to answer in the affirmative."

The solution of this momentous question can only be obtained from the accounts of subsequent visitors; and the following narrative is submitted to the public, as a contribution to the evidence required for that purpose. It was drawn up partly from the papers,† but chiefly from the recital of the author; and the editor has adhered as closely as the nature of the case would permit, to the language in which they were originally related. The intervention of a third person between the traveller and the reader, is an

* Dr. Douglas, Bishop of Salisbury.

† For some account of these papers, see Note A.

evil which ought always, if possible, to be avoided; but in the present instance, some literary assistance was absolutely necessary; and the editor conceives he shall best have executed the task he has imposed upon himself, by stating, with strict fidelity, and in the simplest language, the facts as they were related to him.

A short account of the life of the narrator will enable the reader to judge of the necessity of such assistance, as well as of his qualifications to relate the incidents of his voyage.

ARCHIBALD CAMPBELL was born at Wynford, near Glasgow, on the 19th of July, 1787. His father, who was a soldier in the 45th regiment, died at St. Lucia, upon which his mother removed to Paisley, her native place, when her son was about four years of age. He there received the common rudiments of education, and at the age of ten was bound apprentice to a weaver. Before the term of his apprenticeship had expired, however, a strong desire to visit remote countries induced him to go to sea; and in the year 1800, he entered as apprentice on board the ship Isabella, of Port-Glasgow, commanded by Mr. Hugh Paterson. In this vessel he made three voyages to the West-Indies. He afterwards served about a twelvemonth in a coaster; and, in 1804, again sailed for the West-Indies, in the sloop Robina, belonging to the same port.

At Madeira he was pressed on board the Diana frigate, and remained in that ship till her arrival at Portsmouth in 1806. He there found means to make his escape, and entered as seaman on board the Thames Indiaman.

The history of the six most eventful years of his life will be found in the following pages. He returned to his native country, in April, 1812, having lost both his feet;

and from the unskilful manner in which amputation has been performed, the wounds have never healed.

A gentleman in Rio Janeiro, of the name of Lawrie, had furnished him with letters to his father in Edinburgh, by whose interest he obtained admission into the Infirmary in that city; but after remaining there nearly four months, he was dismissed as incurable.

Mr. Lawrie, senior, presented him with a barrel organ; and he contrived to earn a miserable pittance, by crawling about the streets of Edinburgh and Leith, grinding music, and selling a metrical history of his adventures.

Being ambitious, however, of performing on a more dignified instrument, he has since learned to play on the violin; and he finds employment on board the steam-boats that ply upon the river Clyde, by playing for the amusement of the steerage passengers.

In one of these vessels his appearance attracted the notice of the editor; and the answers he gave to some questions excited so much curiosity, that he took him home with the intention of making a few memoranda of his story for his own information.

The modest and intelligent manner in which it was told, the interesting nature of the incidents, and the curious information it contained, on the subjects to which the attention of the editor had been much directed, created a strong interest on behalf of the narrator; and the hope that an account of his voyage might be of service to an unfortunate and deserving man, and not unacceptable to those who take pleasure in contemplating the progress of mankind in the arts of civilization, gave rise to the present publication.

In the execution of his task, simplicity and perspicuity are all that the editor has aimed at. The ornaments of style, which are generally misplaced in such relations, would have been peculiarly incongruous in the mouth of a common sailor. In those parts of the work which relate to places already well known, the narrative is entirely confined to the personal adventures of the author; and had the editor been aware that so much had been recently written regarding Kamschatka and the Aleutian Islands by the Russian navigators, the description of those places would have been either altogether omitted, or much more condensed; but, in fact, he had no opportunity of seeing their voyages till the work was sent to the press, and it was not then considered necessary to make any alteration in the text.

The importance of the subject will account for the disproportion of that part which relates to the Sandwich Islands to the rest of the work. From the advantages they owe to their situation, placed midway between the continents of Asia and America; from the fertility of the soil, and the natural talents and industry of the natives, they promise to become by far the most important of the recently discovered islands* in the Pacific Ocean.

Scarcely thirty years have elapsed from the period of their discovery, yet how wonderful the change!† Their

* The concluding sentence in Captain Cook's journal affords a striking proof of the high value he attached to "a discovery, which, though the last, seemed in many respects the most important of any that had hitherto been made by Europeans throughout the extent of the Pacific Ocean.

† A short historical account of the revolutions that have taken place in the Sandwich Islands, from their discovery in 1779, till the arrival of the author in 1809, collected from the voyages of Cook, Meares, Portlocke, Vancouver, Broughton, Turnbull, and Lisianski, will be found in the Appendix, No. IV.

king is surrounded by workmen of every description, native and European; his guards are regularly trained to the use of fire arms; and he possesses a navy of nearly sixty sail of decked vessels, built upon the islands; whilst almost every ship which navigates the Pacific, finds shelter, provisions, or trade, in his harbors.

In Tamaahmaah these islanders possess one of those remarkable characters, who, like Alfred or Peter the Great, seems destined to hasten the progress of civilization. He is known in this country from the accounts of Turnbull, Lisianski, and Langsdorf; but as none of these navigators ever saw that chief, their accounts are consequently very imperfect; the length of time, however, during which our author remained in his family, afforded him opportunities of observation not enjoyed by those of higher qualifications, and in some measure compensates for the unavoidable defects of his education.

Although no new discoveries, strictly speaking, are recorded, the work will not be found altogether destitute of useful nautical information; the account of the reef to the southwest of Halibut Island, upon which the ship was wrecked, and the numerous rocks that lie near the coast of Aliaski, will show what ought to be avoided; and in the account of the south coast of Wahoo, will be found a description of the only harbours in the Sandwich Islands.

From the humble situation held by the author, a distrust may be entertained of his qualifications to relate the facts which fell under his notice; but few, in the same ranks of life, are possessed of more intelligence or information; with the advantages common to his countrymen, he seems to have neglected no means of improvement. It will be seen that at the age of nineteen he was appointed a petty officer, and had he not been incapacitated by his misfortune, it may be presumed, that he would soon have attained a higher rank.

The editor has to claim indulgence on his own account. His motives for undertaking the work, and the principles upon which it has been executed, have been already stated; the work is published for the benefit of the poor fellow who is the subject of it; nor would it ever have met the public eye, had there been any chance that the task would have been undertaken by another hand But to rescue much of what is true and extraordinary from the oblivion to which the obscure condition and limited powers of the narrator would have condemned it, appeared to him well deserving of the labour which he had bestowed. The best apology for the appearance of the work itself will be found in the words of a celebrated periodical publication.* "It is obvious that the discovery of new tribes, and the first account of manners formerly unknown, are by no means more interesting than the subsequent history of those tribes, and the changes which rapidly take place in their manners. The greatest obligations, therefore, are conferred upon us by those adventurous persons who, having visited these islands of late years, give such statements of what they saw, as enable us to trace the progress of society in one of its earliest stages, and to estimate the effects produced by the sudden revolution in their circumstances which the natives have experienced from their intercourse with Europeans."

JAMES SMITH.

Jordonhill, May, 1816.

* Edinburgh Review, Vol. IX. p. 332.

VOYAGE

ROUND THE WORLD.

CHAPTER I.

Departure from England—Voyage to China—Transactions at Canton—Author enters on board an American ship—Passage to Kamschatka—Touches at Japan—Transactions there—Arrives at the harbour of St. Peter and St. Paul—Some account of the Russian settlement in that place.

Early in May, 1806, I entered as seaman on board the Thames Indiaman, Matthew Riches, Esq. commander, on a voyage to China.

We sailed on the 14th of that month from Motherbank, in company with the Arniston, Royal Charlotte, Glatton, Marquis of Ely, Marquis of Wellesley, Monarch, Cirencester, and Neptune, Indiamen, under convoy of the Lion, 64, and Medusa frigate; we were also accompanied by a fleet of transports, with troops, destined for the expedition to Buenos Ayres.

In our voyage to the Cape of Good Hope, no incident occurred worthy of being recorded, not even the ordinary ceremonies upon crossing the line. We had a detachment of the 30th regiment on board, the commanding officer of which did not choose that the men should undergo the ducking usual upon that occasion. About this time I was appointed sail-maker's mate.

We arrived at the Cape on the 7th of August, and remained there 15 days,

We sailed from thence on the 22d; and on the day after our departure, encountered a severe gale of wind. It came on so suddenly that we had only time to take in our studding sails; all the others, except the fore and foretop gallant sails, were blown out of the bolt ropes; the ship was running before the wind, and broached to several times; fortunately, however, we suffered no other damage than the loss of the sails. We experienced two other gales whilst in the Indian seas, but, being better prepared, met with no material accident.

On the 12th of September we saw the island of St. Paul, and arrived at Pulo Penang, or Prince of Wales' Island, about the middle of October.

We proceeded on our voyage for China on the 24th of November, and anchored at Wampoa on the 18th of January, 1807.

Having remained there nearly six weeks, and taken in about half of our cargo, an unfortunate dispute took place between the crew of the Neptune and some Chinese, in which one of the latter lost his life. In consequence of this, the government insisted that a man should be given up in his place, and stopped the loading of the ships to enforce compliance with this demand, threatening, at the same time, to prevent their departure by choking up the second bar.* As a measure of precaution the ships dropped down the river below the bar, and a boat was despatched to Canton to wait the orders of the commodore.

I was sent in the cutter on this service; and during the time of our stay in that city, the captain of the American ship Arthur, bound to Rhode-Island, endeavored to induce me to quit the ship I belonged to, by offering high wages, and a bounty of twenty dollars; I, however, declined his proposals. Afterwards, when I was in company with a

* For an account of the dispute, see Appendix, No. IV. Note B.

comrade of the name of Allen, we were met by another American captain, who also tried to persuade us, by offering still higher wages; we resisted his offers, till he informed us that his ship was bound for the South Seas and the north west coast of America.—It had always been my ambition to visit those distant parts of the world, and the opportunity that now presented itself was too tempting to be resisted. We agreed to his terms; and as his ship lay at Wampoa, he concealed us in the American factory till an opportunity of proceeding thither should occur.

Whilst at this place, we very narrowly escaped detection. Being in want of provisions, we sent out a Chinese to buy some bread, and gave him a dollar stamped with Captain Riches' initials. Instead of fulfilling his commission, he took the dollar to the captain, and brought him to the factory. When we saw them approach, we made our escape from a window to the top of an adjoining house, and ran along the roofs, till we reached a warehouse, which we asked permission to pass through; this the owner refusing, I went out on a beam that crossed the street, and dropped on the ground, being a fall of about eighteen feet.—When the Chinese observed this, he allowed my comrade to pass through the house. I was a good deal stunned with the fall, but soon recovered myself. We then got to the river side, where we hired a *san-pan*, or small boat, to take us to Wampoa, and reached the ship with no other interruption.

She was called the Eclipse, and belonged to Boston; a new ship, on her first voyage, commanded by Captain Joseph O'Kean. She was chartered by the Russian American Company, for their settlements at Kamschatka, and the northwest coast of America, with a cargo of nankeens, tea, silks, sugar, rice, and other articles, the produce of China. The number of the crew, including officers, amounted to twenty-eight, four or five of which were procured from the Indiamen. There was also a Russian supercargo.

At Captain O'Kean's desire I changed my name, which I entered on the ship's books as Archibald Macbride.

Having completed our cargo, the ship sailed on her voyage upon the eighth of May.—When opposite to Macao, we saw the Indian fleet getting under way; the Captain, fearing that the man-of-war might board us, and take the men belonging to the India ships, put back, and remained within the Bocca Tigris till they were out of sight.

On the 6th of June we descried the coast of Japan, and ran along shore till we reached the bay of Nangasaki.

We stood into the bay under Russian colors, and were met by an immense fleet of boats, who took possession of the ship, and towed her to the anchorage. When about half way up the bay, the Dutch ambassador came off. He could speak English; and finding we were Americans, advised us to haul down the colors, informing us that the natives were much exasperated at some outrages lately committed by the Russians upon their islands. We found this to be so much the case, that we deemded it prudent to keep the supercargo out of sight during the whole of our stay.*

* It appears from Dr Langsdorf's Voyage, that the *amour propre* of the Russian ambassador, Von Resanoff, was so much mortified by his reception at Japan, that he despatched in October, 1806, an expedition against the most southern of the Kurile islands, where the Japanese have settlements. A second expedition was undertaken in May, 1807.—*Vide Langsdorf, Vol. II. p.* 298.

When the ship was moored, eight guard-boats were anchored round us, within pistol-shot, and no person allowed to land or hold any communication with the shore; the muskets were taken out of the arm-chests, and our gunpowder demanded; six or eight kegs were given up, with the assurance that it was all we had.

Seeing so many boats come off, a large assortment of articles of trade was brought on deck, but none of the people would make any purchase. They told us they had plenty of every thing we had to offer.

When the captain was asked what brought him to Japan, he replied, want of water and fresh provisions; and ordered several butts in the hold to be started and hoisted on deck empty. Next day a plentiful supply was sent off, in small boats, filled with water, and in tubs, which we were obliged to empty on deck, stopping the scuppers, and allowing it to run off at night. We were also abundantly supplied with fresh fish, hogs, and vegetables; the whole of which was furnished gratis.

On the third day of our stay, the Captain, finding nothing was to be gained by remaining, got under way. The arms and ammunition were immediately restored, and the ship was towed about five miles out of the bay, by nearly a hundred boats; on parting the crews cheered us, waving their hats and hands.

The town of Nangasaki was concealed by an island; but from the view we had of the land, it seemed to be in a state of high cultivation, and very populous. The natives have the appearance and complexion of the Chinese, but are taller in stature.

Their boats, which were open, with small covered cabins abaft, were mounted with guns, about the size of our largest swivels. Instead of being rowed they were sculled; the oars on each side never being lifted out of the water. In each of them were two men, apparently officers, dressed in loose frocks or gowns, with long hanging sleeves. These were armed with matchlocks, and had a sabre hanging at each side.

After leaving Nangasaki, we navigated the strait which separates the principal island of Japan from others that lie to the north: in several places it is not above five miles broad. On each side the country is beautiful, abounding with cultivated fields, woods, villages, and single houses. Frequently, when near the coast, we observed the inhabitants come down to the shore, and make signals, as if to invite us to land; but, after the reception we had already experienced, the captain did not choose to have any further communication with the Japanese.*

At one time, in a thick fog, we were alarmed with the noise of breakers, apparently very near. Upon sounding, we found twenty fathoms, sandy bottom, and immediately let go the anchor. When the haze cleared away, we found ourselves close to a remarkable island or rock, about the size and the height of the craig of Ailsea, in the Frith of Clyde. An archway passed completely through it; and into this the sea rushed with that tremendous noise which had occasioned our late alarm.

In about a week we were clear of the strait, and proceeded on our voyage.

* Those friendly invitations seem to be somewhat inconsistent with the inhospitable character of the Japanese. It is most likely, however, that the author is mistaken in the nature of the signals they made, which were more probably those of reproach than kindness, similar to those captain Saris was assailed with—"Core, core cocori ware,"—"you Coreans, with false hearts."

Vide Quarterly Review, Vol. IV. p. 379.

The 4th of July, being the anniversary of American Independence, was celebrated by a salute. One of the guns having missed fire, the captain took the powder-horn to prime it; in doing which some fire in the gun kindled the powder, and exploded the horn. By this accident his hand was dreadfully scorched and lacerated.

Upon the 6th we descried the two lofty mountains of St. Peter and St. Paul, in Kamschatka.

Owing to foggy weather, it was two days before we discovered the entrance of Awatska bay. We were within the heads on the 8th, and were met by a Russian boat, on board of which was Mr. Meznikoff, commissioner of the store, who piloted us into the harbour of Petrapaulouska, or St. Peter and St. Paul. The ship having been seen off the coast, intelligence had been given of our arrival by people stationed for the purpose at a light-house on the north side of the entrance.

Awatska bay is a spacious basin, 25 or 30 miles in circumference; any part of it would afford safe anchorage, but it has three very fine harbours. That of St. Peter and St. Paul, where we lay, is sheltered from every wind by a projecting woody point; but, owing to the great height of the mountains is subject to heavy squalls.

The entrance to the bay is not above a mile and a half wide, and may be known by several remarkable rocks on the starboard hand going in, somewhat like the needles at the Isle of Wight.

We remained at St. Peter and St. Paul thirty-three days, and discharged nearly one third of our cargo.

The town, although the principal sea-port of the Peninsula of Kamschatka, is nothing more than a miserable village, containing 300 or 400 inhabitants, of whom about two-thirds are Russians and the remainder natives. It is situated on an eminence above the harbour, and, with the exception of the governor's house, consists of huts of one story high, built of logs and covered with thatch. In a few of them the windows are glazed with talc, but more generally the intestine of the seal supplies the place of glass.

The huts of the natives lie below the town towards the shore. They are almost wholly under ground, nothing but the roof being seen, which is long and rounded at the top, resembling a vessel with the bottom upwards.

On a rising ground on the north side of the harbour, near the governor's house, stands an obelisk, erected to the memory of Captain Clerke, the coadjutor of Captain Cook, who died at sea, and was buried at this place. The monument is about sixteen or eighteen feet high, built of hewn stone, with a ship on the top; there were inscriptions on each side, which were much defaced by the weather; and owing to the rail which surrounded the place, we could not get near enough to ascertain in what language they were written.*

The natives are stout made, round-faced, with a yellowish complexion. The men are dressed in skin frocks; the women in a similar dress made of nankeen.

The country round is perfectly barren, and no cultivation of any kind is to be seen, except one or two gardens near the town.

* The inscriptions will be found in Captain Krusenstern's Voyage. The Monument was erected by the officers of his ship, the Nadeshda, near the tree where Captain Clerke was buried.

Krusenstern, Vol. II. p. 203.

They have a few horses and horned cattle; but these are so scarce, that the fresh beef we required was brought from Boltcheresk, a distance of seventy miles.

On the right hand entrance of the bay, and round by the foot of the mountain, the country is covered with wood, chiefly pines.

The town and its neighbourhood are infested with an immense number of the dogs used for sledges in winter. At this season, they are allowed to go at large and find food for themselves. They live almost entirely upon fish, which they obtain either by springing upon them as they lie in the water, or picking them up dead along the shore. In winter, they are fed upon dried fish, which are cured in large open sheds erected for that purpose on the shore, and which, it would appear, they prefer to any other food. Our sailors, by way of amusement, often purloined a few to give to the dogs; in consequence of which kindness, thousands of these hungry creatures watched the landing of our boat, and flocked after us, to the great annoyance of the inhabitants.—This practice became at last so troublesome, that the Russians insisted on our putting an end to it. Their howling every morning at day-break, was so intolerable, as to awaken us even on board the ship.

Boltcheresk, the capital of Kamschatka, is about seventy miles from St. Peter and St. Paul. The communication in the winter season is by sledges drawn by dogs over the snow ; in summer the intercourse is carried on by the river Awatska, which being in some places extremely shallow, boats of a particular construction are made use of. They are formed of light frames of wood, covered with tarpaulin, and are so flat in the bottom that they do not draw above six inches water; they are extremely light, and can easily be carried over the rapids.

The two remarkable mountains, St. Peter and St. Paul, which give name to the place, lie about thirty miles to the north. One of them is a volcano; and when we could see the top, which was seldom free from clouds, it was constantly smoking, and at night sparks were frequently to be seen. An eruption took place some time before our arrival, by which the whole town was covered with ashes.

There were no vessels at this place during our stay, except the wreck of a ship which had sunk in the harbour; the sails having been loosed for the purpose of drying, a sudden squall laid her on her beam-ends, when she filled and went down.* As the upper works were above the surface at low water, it appeared to us that she might have been raised without much difficulty; but it seems they did not mean to make the attempt, for her cordage and anchors were put on board our vessel.

Whilst we remained here we were abundantly supplied with the finest salmon, and fish of all descriptions.

Having delivered the part of our cargo which was to be left at this place, we sailed on the 8th of August for the settlements on the Aleutian Islands.

* It appears from Captain Krusenstern's voyage, that this was the Slawa Rossii, the ship commanded by Captain Billing, and afterwards by Admiral Sarytscheff.

Krusenstern, Vol. II. page 29

CHAPTER II.

Departure from Kamschatka—Shipwrecked on a reef of rocks, on the northwest coast of America—Author, with the rest of the crew, save themselves by the long boat—Are drifted on an island—Transactions upon the island—Prepare to build a vessel.

We left Kamschatka on the 8th of August, and proceeded on our voyage to the north-west coast of America. Nothing material occurred till the 10th of September. On the morning of that day it blew hard from the south, and the ship was reduced to close reefed topsails; about three in the afternoon, the gale increased to such a degree that it became necessary to take in the fore and mizen topsails. Whilst the men were on the yards, they discovered land off the lee bow, distant about five or six leagues; we conjectured it to be that part of the continent called Aliaska; the ship's course was immediately altered from N. E. to E. and the weather proving more moderate in the evening, stood on, close hauled, but did not set more sail. About ten at night, the alarm was given that there were breakers ahead, and on the lee bow. Mr. Brinkman, the chief mate, who had the charge of the watch, immediately went to the mizen topmast head, and observing there was room to wear the ship, hastened below to report the circumstance to the captain. When he returned upon deck, he instantly went to the wheel and ordered us to our stations, with the intention of wearing; but the captain, who followed him, was of a different opinion; he said what we saw was only white water, and not breakers; that there was no danger, and ordered us to stand on our course. He had scarcely given this order before the ship plunged, and struck with such violence as to knock away the fore-foot, and the watch below were driven from their hammocks against the deck. The sea running very high, she beat so hard that in a few minutes the rudder was unshipped, and the stern-post forced up through the poop; as she still had way upon her, she shot over the reef into deep water: upon sounding we found seventeen fathoms. It was immediately determined to let go the anchor, and remain by the ship as long as she would swim. In case she went down, we hoped to save our lives by the long-boat, which was accordingly cleared and hoisted out, that she might be ready; seven of the guns were at the same time thrown overboard, in order to keep her above water until daylight. The carpenter attempted to sound the well, but owing to some obstacle, could not get down the sounding rod. I was sent below with him to bore a hole beside the pump thro' the lower deck; but on taking off the after hatch, we found the water as high as the shifting boards.

Early on the morning of the 11th, to our great joy, we saw land to the leeward of us, distant about three or four leagues. It was immediately determined to watch the lull, slip the cable, and cast the ship's head in shore, and steer her for it with the jib and fore-topsail.— After she was under way, the captain ordered that any of the crew that could not swim should go into the long-boat astern, and be ready as soon as she struck to come alongside for the rest, as he expected that she would then go to pieces. As soon as she struck, all hands came into the boat, and went for the shore, the captain taking his quadrant, until the tide should ebb, when he expected she would be nearly dry. We landed between eleven and twelve o'clock in the forenoon.

The land upon which we were thrown presented a most dreary appearance; it was an extensive plain, intersected by pools of fresh water, stretching about five miles from the sea, and terminated by two mountains. The ground was covered with heath and moss; not a tree nor a bush could be seen, neither did we observe the least trace of human habitations. As the land afforded us no sustenance, we turned our attention to the sea, and when the tide ebbed found some large muscles.—Having satisfied our hunger with some raw muscles, we prepared to go off to the ship; but on our way off we had the mortification to see her fall over on her beam ends. When we reached the ship we found that we could do nothing with her, and were preparing to leave her, when we discovered in the bottom of the long-boat the carpenter's axe; we then cut the parrel and gear of the main-topsail yard, and let it drive clear of the wreck, while we went to cut away the topmasts, and then left her for that day. On our way ashore we found the main-topsail yard, and took it in tow, and landed again about six o'clock in the evening.

The approach of night rendering some shelter necessary, we made a sort of tent with a sail, and lay down on the moss, cold and wet, and spent a most uncomfortable night.

Next morning, the 12th, we set off along shore in search of any thing that might have driven from the ship, and found, in a bay at no great distance from our tent, a barrel of rosin, the arm chest, with one or two small carbines, some swan-shot, and, what was of greater consequence to us, several calking irons and mallets; on finding these we went to the ship, but the sea was so high we could not come near her, and we returned to our tent.

On the 13th, 14th, and 15th, we were employed in repairing the boat, which had begun to get very leaky; having picked some oakum, we calked the seams as well as we could. Over the places where this was insufficient, we nailed pieces of boards, and calked round the edges. Although we could not pay the seams, having nothing to melt our rosin in, we succeeded in making her tolerably tight.

On the 16th several pieces of wreck and some sails were secured; this day was chiefly employed in preparations for going off to the wreck.

We formed a grappling iron by lashing four bolts together, and bending them, and made a line out of the rigging that came ashore with the spars; this proved of great service in fishing up articles from the wreck. Every thing being ready, and the 17th proving fine, we set off at day-break, and taking the carpenter's axe with us, we cut a large hole in her side, just before the main channels.—With the grappling irons we hooked several sails, and a number of other articles, such as boxes of silks and nankeens, and made three different trips to the wreck this day.

On the 18th we were busy in making a larger tent with the sails we had got. We set up two small spars at each end, and laid a studding sail boom across the tops of them; over this we spread a topsail, hung smaller sails at the ends, and placed planks round the bottom, to prevent them from being blown up by the wind. With the soft moss of the island for beds, and planks to sit upon, we now found ourselves pretty comfortable in every respect but one: All our attempts to kindle a fire proved unavailing, and we were obliged to eat our victuals raw. Observing a flight of large birds, resembling ravens, carrying something in their talons, we watched where they alighted, and going to the spot, found several parcels of pork and beef which they had picked up, the barrels being staved by the rocks. In this manner we procured about a dozen of pieces. We again went off to the wreck in the afternoon, to see what we could get on shore, as it had every appearance of a gale of wind, and managed to get three of our chests out of the vessel before dark; and amongst them mine. It contained only one shirt and my bible, which I had put into one of those squares, common in sailor's chests, for holding case bottles, and in which it was firmly fixed, in consequence of having swelled with the water. I was at great pains in drying it in the sun, and succeeded so well that I could read any part of it. It was afterwards saved from a second wreck; and in my future hardships and sufferings, the perusal of it formed my greatest consolation. It is still in my possession, being the only article I brought with me when I returned to my native country.

We also secured this day, a barrel of fine biscuit; it was soaked with salt water, but was, nevertheless, a most acceptable addition to our store. In the night, between the 18th and 19th, it blew so hard from the south, that the ship went to pieces before morning. At day-break, we discovered on a small isle, separated from the land by a channel which was dry at low water, the fore part of the ship, which had driven high up on the beach. Had we been able to have moved it to a better situation, it would have made an excellent hut; but this was beyond our strength. It was broken up and gradually removed when we could afford time. Some more fragments of the wreck, consisting of knees and planks, came on shore this day. We also recovered a few packages of nankeens and chests of tea, which we spread on the moss to dry.

Our horizon to the south being interrupted by the reef, the captain and mate went out in the long-boat to determine the latitude by a meridian altitude of the sun. The result of the observations gave 54 deg. 52 min. north, as the latitude of the south side of the island.*

* This observation, made without the assistance of an ephemeris, or tables of declination, can only be considered as an approximation It however proves that Sannack and Halibut island is the same, the latitude of that island, as ascertained by captain Cook, being 54 deg. 27 min. As the observation was made about the time of the equinox, the correction for declination might be estimated within a few minutes.

We made a number of trips to the wreck in the course of the ten following days, and saved a considerable part of the cargo, consisting of chests of tea, packages of nankeens, and bags of rice. The last time we went off to the wreck, before the arrival of the Indians, the wind was off shore, and began to blow so fresh that we were obliged to desist from our labours. After having secured a few more sails, some coils of cordage, and two bales of silks, having only two oars and a heavy boat to row, we reached the shore before dark, after a most fatiguing pull. By this time so much of the wreck was recovered that we determined to build a vessel large enough to carry us to the Sandwich Islands, where we were certain of meeting with an American ship. Our principal attention was now turned to that object, and we began our preparations by collecting into one place planks and other pieces of wood suitable for the purpose.

CHAPTER III.

Arrival of a party of Natives, and of the Russian Commandant of Oonalaska, who determines to send to Kodiak for assistance—Long-boat prepared for the voyage—Some account of Sannack or Halibut Island.

Our necessary occupations, and the unpromising appearance of the country, had hitherto prevented us from leaving the neighbourhood of our hut; but we had seen nothing that led us to imagine that the island was inhabited. We were, however, visited on the 28th, by a party of natives, who had traced the fragments of wreck along shore.

About mid-day we saw them approach in three small skin canoes, with one Indian in each. One of them, who had a gold medal about his neck, came forward, and addressed us in the Russian language. The captain, who had made a former voyage to these settlements, and understood a few words of the language, contrived to make our situation known to him. He immediately despatched one of his companions to a village on the northern part of the island for assistance, and the other to Oonalaska to give information to the commandant of the Russian settlements on that island.

The chief himself remained, and most willingly gave us a share of his provisions, which consisted of a bladder of train oil, and a basket of berries, about the size of bilberries, preserved in oil. These, to people in any other situation, would scarcely have been deemed an acquisition. Even we, who had lived so long on raw muscles, found some difficulty in reconciling ourselves to train oil; but we thought the berries, which had been cured with seal oil, no small luxury. This friendly Indian, who had hooks and lines, went out in his canoe, and in a short time returned with a few small fish. He then kindled a fire in the following manner: he laid a piece of soft wood upon the ground, and took another within his teeth; between these he put an upright piece of a harder quality, which he twirled rapidly around with a thong of hide, as we would a drill; the friction soon kindled the soft wood, and by placing it in dried grass, and blowing it, it burst into a flame.

We lost no time in broiling the fish, and enjoyed the first comfortable meal we had since the shipwreck.

Next day about forty Indians, men and women, came and encamped beside us; they made huts for themselves, by setting up planks, leaning against each other at the top, and throwing earth upon them, over which they put a covering of grass.

They brought a supply of provisions, consisting of berries, oil, blubber, and dried salmon, and gave us a share of all they had with the utmost liberality.

By the assistance of the Indians, who towed our boat with their canoes, we made two more trips to the wreck, and were successful in saving a considerable quantity of the cargo, as well as several articles of greater use to us for our intended vessel; such as bolts of canvass, cordage, and other naval stores, being part of the rigging of the ship that was stranded in the harbor of St. Peter and St. Paul. In saving these articles, the grappling-irons proved of the greatest service; for though the wreck lay in about three fathoms, the water was so clear, when the wind was southerly, that we could distinctly see what lay at the bottom. A considerable part of the ship still held together.

In about a week after this, Mr. Bander, the Russian commandant of Oonalaska, arrived in a large skin canoe or baidare, with twenty or thirty Indians, who also hutted themselves beside us. The presence of so many visiters formed a singular contrast to the solitude in which we had hitherto lived. Our tent was now in the centre of a busy and populous village.

Some of our new visiters erected huts, whilst others contented themselves with sleeping under their baidare, which they placed bottom up, and raised by supports from the ground on the lee side.

We were now in no want of provisions.—In addition to what the Indians brought with them, they procured us a plentiful supply of fish and fowl, particularly geese, in which the island abounded; these they shot with their rifles, in the use of which they are very expert.

These rifles are no wider in the bore than our own; but the metal is extremely thick, particularly at the muzzle. They load them almost full of powder, over which they force a piece of lead, three or four inches long, with a mallet; this comes out like an arrow.

The piece is rested upon two supports, which fold out, and are stuck in the ground. I have seen them fire at the geese, which usually sat in rows, and kill several at one shot.

Mr. Bander took possession of the ship's cargo. Under his directions we went off to her several times, in company with the Indians, and brought away a considerable quantity of the nankeens and cloth; but were not successful in getting provisions, for we secured nothing except a few casks of damaged bread, and half a puncheon of rum.

Our chief attention was now turned towards our vessel, and we had a reasonable prospect of completing her by the aid of our visiters.

From Oonalaska we procured twelve Indians who could use the axe, and Mr. Bander promised us the assistance of Russian carpenters from Kodiak. To obtain which, as well as to report the loss of the ship to the governor of the Russian settlements, the long-boat was fitted out for a voyage to Kodiak.—About the 6th of November the necessary repairs were begun.

The seams were payed with a composition of the rosin that had been saved from the wreck, and train oil, boiled to a consistence in the kettles of the Indians. A kind of spar deck was formed, by laying the boards of the hat boxes over the thwarts; and upon these we nailed a tarpaulin: a hatch way was left at the stern, by which we got below, and in which the man at the helm could stand. We laid a small platform on the bottom, and covered it with skins; this formed a birth into which we could creep, but it was too low to allow us to sit upright. Out of the ship's spanker I made a suit of sails. She was rigged a sloop, and provided with a cable and grapnel. She was small enough for a voyage of 500 miles at such a season, being only twenty-two feet long, and measuring about six ton. She, however, proved an excellent sea-boat.

Every thing being completed by the 17th, we laid in our stores, consisting of dried salmon, berries, and oil, with a cask of water, and sailed on the following morning. The crew consisted of Mr. Bartram, second mate, myself, and seven more of the crew, one Indian, who acted as pilot.

The island on which we had now remained two months, is called by the natives Sannack; by Captain Cook it is named Halibut Island. It is situated in latitude 54. 27. north, longitude 197. east, and lies 10 or 12 leagues to the south of the promontory of Aliaski, and about 60 east of Oonalaska. It is quite flat, with the exception of two mountains, is eight or ten miles long, and about six broad. The main land could be distinctly seen; and the remarkable volcano mentioned by Captain Cook, bore N. N. W. from our tent. It was constantly smoking during the day, and at night we could frequently see the flames.

The land produces nothing eatable but berries. To the south lies the dangerous reef upon which we were wrecked; it is of great extent, for when at the ship we observed breakers a considerable distance to the southward.

There is a village of 12 or 15 Indian families at the northern extremity of the island.—These people are under the government of the Russians, for whom they provide furs for the American company. They are a quite inoffensive race, converts to the Greek Church, and if not very devout, are at least extremely attentive to the ceremonial part of crossing themselves.

Their appearance and manners will be afterwards more particularly described. As the whole of their sustenance, clothing, and, indeed, every article they make use of, except a few berries, are the produce of the sea, they are extremely expert in managing their canoes, and most ingenious in their modes of catching fish and other sea animals. They are excellent marksmen with the rifle and spear; to the latter they fix a bladder, which prevents the wounded animal from taking it under water, and dart it with great force and certainty by means of a throwing stick.

Like all other savages I have seen, they are immoderately fond of spirits and tobacco.

CHAPTER IV.

Sail from Sannack in the long-boat—Touch at the Island of Ungar—Distressing state of the settlement there—Sail from thence—Anchor at the village of Schutkum—Departure from it—Boat nearly embayed on the north coast of Kodiak—Arrived at Alexandria—Transactions there—Boat fitted out to return to Sannack.

We sailed from Sannack, in the long-boat, on the morning of the 18th of November; but had scarcely been an hour at sea, before we discovered a leak in the counter, which forced us to put back.

Having repaired the damage, we again set sail next morning, with a fair southerly wind. Our little vessel made better weather than could have been expected, and so long as it continued moderate, she scudded before the sea perfectly dry; we boomed out the foresail on the weather side, and the wind being fair, proceeded on our voyage at a great rate.—About noon it freshened into a smart gale, and the sea rose considerably, frequently curling over the stern in an alarming manner. Our open cock-pit rendered this extremely dangerous, till we adopted an expedient of which I fortunately recollected having read in the voyages of some Dutch navigators, who used oil to smooth the sea. Upon trying the experiment, it proved an effectual remedy. We lashed a keg of oil upon the taffrail, allowing a small stream to run from it, which spread a scum over the surface in our wake, and completely prevented the waves from topping.

The coast of Aliaski which we passed this day, is very mountainous, and deeply indented with arms of the sea. Many small islands lie near the shore, which are covered with brushwood. Sometimes a temporary hut erected by the hunters is to be seen, but there were no other symptoms of inhabitants. Extensive reefs of rocks lie a considerable distance off the land; our pilot, who was well acquainted with the navigation, took us within them; but strangers should be very cautious in approaching this part of the coast.

About ten at night we were close in with an island of considerable height, and attempted to pass to leeward, but were prevented by breakers, which obliged us to tack and pass on the outside. A round lofty rock lies a quarter of a mile to the southwest; the channel within seemed also full of rocks, and we were obliged to make another tack before we could weather it. Our situation for about two hours after this, was very alarming; we passed many sunk rocks, and were repeatedly obliged to tack in order to avoid them.

At day-break we found ourselves near a barren island, four or five miles in length, lying to the south of a larger one called Ungar. We passed through the sound between them, and, coasting along the southern shore of Ungar, arrived about ten A. M. at a village, situated on the eastern part of the island, after a run of 160 miles.

We found the settlement here in the most distressing situation. The whole of the male inhabitants, except the Russian overseer and his son, and the Indian interpreter, having gone out to catch seals, about three weeks before this time, a severe gale of wind came on, which their slight canoes were unable to resist, and every one of them perished. This dreadful calamity did not prevent the survivors from receiving us with the kindest hospitality. We were lodged in the hot bath, which was effectually warmed by the steam of water thrown upon red-hot stones.

Ungar is nearly twenty miles in length; in the interior the country rises into lofty mountains; near the sea it is more level, and is covered with brushwood, but produces no vegetable food, except berries, and a root from which the Russians make the liquor called quass. We remained eight days at this place, during which we went out several times to shoot deer, with which the island abounds, accompanied by the son of the overseer and the interpreter; we had tolerable sport, and the venison made a most acceptable addition to our store.

The natives seem, in all respects, the same as those at Sannack. The settlement consisted of one Russian and about thirty Indian families. The houses of the latter were built of mud, in the form of a bee-hive, with a hole at the top instead of a door; they had no fire-places, but warmed themselves by means of lamps made out of flat hollow stones, with rush wicks, which when cold, they placed under their frocks. One cooking place served for the whole village.

This island is separated from the main land, by a strait nearly ten miles wide at high water, but so extremely shallow that it is said to dry at low ebbs, when deer frequently pass over from the continent.

The village is situated on the north side of a small, well sheltered harbour, the entrance to which is between two rocky heads, not above a cable's length asunder. Within it is a quarter of a mile broad, and divides, a short way above the village, into two branches, one of which extends a considerable distance to the west. There are three or four high pointed rocks a little to the south of the entrance, but there is deep water all round.

We sailed on the morning of the 28th, with the wind at N. W. and steered between the main land and a small isle to the east of Ungar. Before we reached the open sea, the wind headed us, and blew with such violence as to force us back to the harbour we left in the morning. Gales from the N. E. with heavy falls of snow, prevented us from sailing for the eight following days. I employed myself in making a squaresail out of a bolt of canvass we had for the purpose.

Having laid in a store of deer's flesh, dried and boiled, the only provisions the place afforded, we again sailed on the morning of the

6th of December; the wind strong from the west, with squalls, accompanied with snow showers. The excessive cold made us feel severely the want of a camboose, or fire place in the boat.

We continued to coast along the main land, within half a mile of the shore. Nothing could exceed the barren aspect of the country, which consisted of a range of steep and rugged hills, destitute of wood, or almost any appearance of vegetation. Many reefs lie a considerable way off the land.

On the 7th we passed an island called St. Ivan, the weather still very cold, with snow.

In the afternoon, the wind veered to the N. E. and blew with such violence that we were driven out to sea; had the gale continued, our situation would have been highly critical; for our water was nearly expended, and we were unprovided with a compass to direct our course; fortunately, however, it abated towards morning, when we tacked and stood to the shore. About noon we were close in with the land, and being anxious to kindle a fire, anchored in a bay, where the brushwood grew down to the water's edge. One of the Indians landed to cut firewood, but he was scarcely upon shore when three bears made their appearance, and forced him to swim back to the boat. We were reluctantly obliged to desist; and having weighed anchor, we went ten miles further, to a village called Schutcum.

A number of sunk rocks lie about half a mile to the south of this place, with an intricate and narrow channel, through which we were piloted by the overseer, who came out to meet us in a bidarka.

After remaining here three days, we sailed again on the 13th, having met with the same hospitable treatment we had uniformly experienced from these islanders. They liberally supplied us with berries and oil, bear's flesh, and dried salmon. Soon after leaving Schutcum, we doubled a bluff head, and opened up a strait* that separates Kodiak from the main land; a short way beyond it passed a narrow entrance leading into a spacious bay or inlet; the pilot told us that it stretched twenty or thirty verst† into the

* Captain Mears, in the Snow Nootka, navigated this strait in 1786; he named it Petrie's Strait. In the chart affixed to Coxe's Russian Discoveries, and by Dr. Langsdorf, it is named the Strait of Chelekoff.

† A verst is about two thirds of a mile.

country, and afforded an excellent shelter for ships. We then stood over to Kodiak, which we reached in the evening; the wind W. S. W. with fine weather; we run along shore during the night. Next day, about two o'clock, we passed near a rock, on which several outches, or sea-lions, were sitting; some of them swam towards us, uttering loud yells; but as the boat was going at a great rate through the water, we soon lost sight of them.

Soon after, whilst crossing a deep bay, the wind checked round to the northwest, and blew so hard at times as to oblige us to take in all our sails. We endeavored to run under the west point of the bay, where there seemed to be good shelter; but we fell to leeward, and were under apprehensions that we should not be able to weather the point that formed its eastern extremity. Mr. Bertram proposed to run the boat ashore, but the surf was so heavy, that the attempt would have been extremely hazardous. I was of opinion that we might weather the point by carrying sail, and he allowed me to take the helm. Having set our close-reefed mainsail and storm-jib, the whole crew, except myself, went below, and lay as much as possible to the weather side, by which means the boat was enabled to carry sail till we cleared the head. After this we had the wind upon our quarter, and the evening proving fine, we made great progress.

The channel or strait, which separates Kodiak from the continent, is about fifteen leagues in breadth, and as far as I could judge, is free from danger, except close in shore.

We entered by moonlight the strait between Kodiak and several smaller islands to the east, with a strong tide in our favor, and were clear of it before daylight.

Being in want of water, we landed early in the morning, and having kindled a fire, had a warm breakfast before embarking.—The country here was well wooded with pines, but we saw no inhabitants. We made sail about eleven, and entered the harbour of Alexandria before dark. We hoisted a Russian jack which we had on board, upon which a Baiderai came off and towed us in. There were two ships and a brig at anchor in the bay.

Alexandria is the principal Russian settlement in the Fox islands, and the residence of the governor, upon whom we waited immediately upon our landing, with our letters from Mr. Bander.

He gave each of us a tumbler of brandy, and sent us to the cazerne, or barracks, where the Russian convicts lodged.

The brig which lay in the harbour was ordered to be fitted out for Sannack, for the purpose of taking in that part of the cargo of the Eclipse which had been saved from the wreck. As it would take a considerable time before she could be got ready, the governor ordered us to return in the boat with the carpenters and tools required for our vessel, that no time might be lost.

We remained here three weeks, and during that time we were employed in preparations for our return. The boards we had nailed on the boat's bottom were stripped off, and she was thoroughly repaired by the Russian carpenters. A camboose for our fire was made, by sawing a cask in two, and filling it with gravel, and secured by lashing it to the mast. We also provided ourselves with a compass, the want of which we had experienced in our voyage thither, our view of the land having been almost constantly intercepted by fogs and snow showers.

Mr. Baranoff, the governor, gave us a chart of the Fox islands and adjoining continent; and furnished us with letters, in case we should find it necessary to touch at any of the Russian settlements; he also sent three carpenters to assist in the construction of our vessel.

By the 8th of January 1808, every thing was completed, and we had laid in a good stock of provisions, consisting of salted pork and bear's flesh, two skin bags of rusk, two casks of water, and a keg of rum, with preserved berries, and blubber for the Indians.

CHAPTER V.

Departure from Alexandria—Boat forced into a bay by the weather, and hauled on shore—Obliged, by want of provisions, to leave the bay—A snow storm—The boat springs aleak—Is run on shore, and goes to pieces upon the rocks—A hut discovered, in which the crew pass the night.

We quitted the harbour of Alexandria on the morning of the 9th of January, (O. S.)* on our voyage back to Halibut island.

With a fine breeze of southerly wind we coasted along the northeast shore of Kodiak, leaving on our right a cluster of islands which lie to the eastward. Upon the largest, which is called Afognac, I was informed there are several Russian settlements.

This is the finest part of the island I have seen, the country being covered with wood, chiefly of the pine tribe, and many of the trees of great size. The other islands are also well wooded.

In the evening the wind died away, and the tide turned against us when nearly half

* The dates in this part of the work, are according to the Russian style.

way through the straits. We anchored for the night in a cove on the larboard side.

Next morning at daylight, we weighed, with a strong breeze from the east, which soon carried us clear of the strait. Upon reaching the open sea, we shaped our course to the northwest.

The headland or cape, which forms the extremity on the starboard hand, is perfectly level on the summit for nearly a mile, and terminates in a lofty perpendicular cliff.

On the following day the wind changed to the northwest, and blew hard, with a heavy sea; as it was directly against us, with every appearance of a gale coming on, we were obliged to bear away for a harbour. At noon, we reached a well sheltered bay, on the northern side of Kodiak. From the threatening appearance of the weather, it was judged prudent to haul the boat on shore; and there being no habitations within reach, we were under the necessity of living on board.

The bay was surrounded by high mountains, with a rocky shore, except at our landing place, where there was a small extent of sandy beach. The whole country was at this time, many feet deep with snow, which prevented us from making any distant excursions. At this place we were forced by the weather to remain ten days.

The dread of famine at last obliged us to put to sea, although the state of the weather was by no means favourable for the prosecution of our voyage. The surrounding country produced no food of any kind, and our stock of provisions was nearly expended. We left the bay, in hopes of reaching a settlement called Karlouski, which lay at no great distance to the west.

We launched the boat on the morning of the 21st, and stood over towards the main land. When about mid-channel, we discovered that the boat had sprung a leak; at the same time a heavy fall of snow came on, accompanied with violent squalls. The leak gained so much upon us, that it became absolutely necessary to run for the nearest shore. —Had the day been clear, we might have got back to the harbour we had quitted in the morning; but the snow rendered it so dark that we could scarcely see a boat's length ahead; we had therefore no resource but to put before the wind, and trust our lives to Providence.

The first view we had of the shore was most alarming; we were completely embayed, with a heavy surf breaking amongst the rocks, whilst, at the same time, the violence of the gale, and the state of the boat, were such as to preclude any hopes of working out of the bay. We therefore turned the bow to that part of the shore which seemed clearest of rocks, and a sea carried us so far up, that when it retired, we were left almost dry; the next wave carried us a little further, upon which the second mate imprudently let go the anchor; when it retired we all jumped out, and reached the shore in safety. Upon the return of the swell, the boat swung round, with her head to the sea, and being prevented by the anchor from driving farther up, she almost immediately went to pieces upon the rocks.

That part of the island on which we were cast was quite barren, and many miles distant from the nearest settlement, the path to which lay across mountains covered with snow.

After collecting what we could save of the wreck of the boat, we set out in search of some place to shelter us for the night, and fortunately discovered, at no great distance, one of those huts that are constructed for the use of the fox and bear hunters. It was too small to admit of a fire in the inside; but the number of people crowded into it rendered the cold less intense; and we lighted a fire in the open air, at which we made ready our provisions.

Upon examining our remaining stock, we found, that with the utmost economy, it would not last above three or four days; it became therefore necessary to form some plan to extricate ourselves from so deplorable a situation.

The bay in which we were wrecked was surrounded with high mountains, which ran down to the shore, terminating in a steep range of rocks, or what sailors call an iron bound coast. Karlouski, the nearest settlement, lay, as we were informed by our Russian companions, at a considerable distance to the west. We deliberated whether we should attempt to reach it by crossing the mountains, or by going along shore at low water. The danger and difficulty of making our journey over the snow deterred us from adopting the first plan: we therefore fixed on the latter, and determined to set out on our journey next morning.

CHAPTER VI.

A party quit the hut in search of a settlement—Author's feet frost-bitten—Progress of the party interrupted by a mountain—Return towards the hut, till prevented by the tide from passing a reef of rocks—Pass the night in a valley—Next morning set off at low water—Author falls behind, and in attempting to climb over a rock, gets his hands frost-bitten—Critical situation—Reaches the hut—Two Russians reach a settlement by the mountains, and send relief—Some account of Karlouski—Voyage to Alexandria.

On the morning of the 22d we quitted the hut, leaving one of the Russians and our Indian pilot to take charge of what we had saved from the boat.

Having proceeded some distance, we were interrupted by a reef of rocks, over which it was necessary to wade. I was provided with strong seal-skin boots, but unfortunately in crossing they were filled with water, which, the cold being so severe, the exercise of walking did not prevent from freezing. In a short time I lost all feeling in my feet, but was able to keep up with my companions, till our progress along shore was completely stopped by a mountain which projected into the sea. Finding it impossible to get round the base, we attempted to climb over the summit. It was very steep, and in many places crusted with ice. I had by this time entirely lost the use of my feet, and with all my exertions, was unable to keep pace with my companions. In many places I was forced to dig steps in the ice and snow, with a pair of boots I had on my hands for that purpose. At length, after great labour and fatigue, I gained what I imagined to be the summit; it proved, however, to be little more than half way up, and the higher part of the mountain was quite inaccessible. I endeavoured to descend again; but in a short time found that the state of my feet rendered the attempt unavailing. I had no alternative but to slide down; and, therefore, throwing away the boots, and placing my hands behind me, to direct my course, I came down with such velocity, that at the foot of the hill, I sunk at least ten feet into the frozen snow. I was at first almost suffocated, till I made a little room by pressing the snow from me. I called as loud as I was able for assistance, but could not make my companions hear me, although I heard their voices perfectly well calling upon me. I at length relieved myself, by compressing the snow till it became sufficiently hard to bear my weight. I then planted my feet into it, and reached the surface.

We turned back, and endeavoured to proceed by a valley which lay behind the mountain. My feet by this time were frozen, never to recover; and I was so ill able to ascend, that I was frequently blown over by the wind, and sometimes driven a considerable way down the hill. Exhausted by these fruitless trials to keep up with the rest, I became totally unable to proceed, and was left to my fate. I laid myself down on the snow in a state of despair. Having recovered a little, I resolved to make another attempt to follow the track of my companions, but had not proceeded far when I met them coming down the hill, which had proved to be impassable.

We now set off on our return to the hut, but were soon interrupted by a steep rock, which the rising tide prevented us from passing. We had no resource but to wait till low water next day, and to pass the night where we were. This was a most unfortunate circumstance for me, for had I reached the hut, and got my feet dried, they would in all likelihood have recovered. It blew hard, and the night was piercingly cold; we therefore returned to the valley, where there was at least some shelter from the wind.

The Russians, who knew the effects of cold, informed us that the consequences of lying down would be fatal. Although well aware of this, I was so much overcome by cold and fatigue, that I several times dropt asleep upon my feet; but my companions, who had not suffered so much, took care to arouse me.

Next morning we again set off for the hut, and met with no interruption till we came to the reef where I had got my feet wet. In consequence of the high wind, the swell was heavier than it had been the day before, and my feet were so powerless that a wave washed me completely off the reef into deep water. It was fortunately towards the shore, and on the returning wave I recovered my footing, and succeeded in getting over.

I followed my companions as well as my exhausted strength and the state of my feet would permit, but fell considerably behind, and had entirely lost sight of them, when my progress was impeded by a projecting crag, through which a natural perforation formed the only passage. The entrance was elevated a considerable way from the ground, and that part of the rock over which it was necessary to scramble, was nearly perpendicular, and almost covered with ice.

With a little assistance I could have easily got over; but situated as I was, my own exertions were of little avail. My feet were of no use in climbing, and I was obliged to drag myself up by my hands, in doing which they also were frozen. After many ineffectual attempts, I had, as I thought, gained the top; but when I had tried to lay hold of a projection in the rock, my fingers refused to perform their office, and I fell to the ground.

The tide was fast rising, and the surge already washed the spot where I stood; in a few minutes it would have been too late, and I must have perished had I been obliged to remain another tide, with my feet and hands frozen, and my whole body wet. As a last resource, I collected a few stones, which I had just strength to pile sufficiently high to enable me to get over.

This took place early in the day, and the hut was only a few miles farther on, but I was so much enfeebled that I did not reach it till dusk.

I never again walked on my feet; but, by the blessing of God, recovered the use of my hands, with the loss of only two fingers.

I was treated with great humanity upon my arrival, by the Russians, who had preserved their clothes dry in seal skin bags. They gave me a suit, and having cut off my boots, wrapped my feet and hands in flannel drawers. I was laid upon a bed of dried grass, after having satisfied my hunger with some rusk and blubber, which were the only provisions that remained.

As our stock was so low, no time was to be lost in procuring assistance; accordingly, the two who had remained set out next morning to endeavor to reach the settlement by the mountains.

On the third day after their departure our provisions were completely exhausted; but the weather had been tolerable, and we knew that if they succeeded, they would lose no time in sending us relief.

On the 27th, those who had been on the look out brought the joyful intelligence that five canoes were in sight, which proved to have been sent by our companions, who had reached the village in safety.

We quitted the hut on the 28th, in the canoes, which were baidarkas, with three seats in each. In crossing a bay we encountered a heavy sea; in order to keep me dry I was put below, and the hole in which I sat was stuffed up with the gut frock.

It was a great relief to me when we got into smoother water, for the space into which I was crammed was so small that I had nearly been suffocated. We arrived at Karlouski in the evening.

This settlement consisted of about thirty Indian families, and several Russians; the latter lived together in a cazerne, and the Indians in huts, which at this place were built of logs, wood being plenty. I was carried to the cazerne, where I was laid upon a bed of skins, and treated with the utmost attention; but as the place afforded no medical assistance, my feet and hands began to mortify, and my health was otherwise so much impaired, that I was frequently in a state of delirium.

We remained here till about the 25th of February, when we took our passage in a baiderai, or large skin-boat, bound to Alexandria, with a cargo of furs, berries, oil, and fish.—

They had for provisions the salmon-roe, preserved in train oil, and kept in bladders. This is by them esteemed a delicacy, but it was too strong for my stomach.

The first night we landed at a village constructed differently from any I had hitherto seen; the whole of the houses, except the roofs, were under ground, and communicated with each other by a subterraneous passage. Bad weather, and contrary winds, detained us at this place eleven days.

We sailed again on the 7th of March. The wind being fair we hoisted a squaresail, and ran before it at a great rate. There is a group of small islands abreast of the south point of North-Island, at which place the tides meet, causing a heavy breaking sea; and as the baiderai was deeply loaded, it had a frightful appearance. The frame of the vessel was so extremely slight, that when between the waves, she was bent into a deep curve, and whilst on the top of the wave the two ends were as much depressed. I was in constant apprehension that the frame would give way. She however, went through the sea drier than a stiffer vessel would have done, and we reached the harbour of Alexandria on the 9th, without any accident.

CHAPTER VII.

Author carried to hospital—Both his feet amputated—Account of the party left at Sannack—Employed in teaching native children English—Account of Kodiak—Natives—Dress—Canoes—Superstition—Food—Author sails in the ship Neva for the Sandwich Islands.

UPON our arrival at Alexandria I was immediately carried to the hospital. The surgeon, on examining my feet, found them in a state of mortification; he used poultices of rye, and other applications, for several days, in hopes of effecting a cure. On the second day he cut off one of my fingers; I lost a joint of another, but all the rest recovered.

Finding no favourable symptoms in my feet, he informed me I must submit to lose them in order to save my life. I had no idea that the case was so hopeless, and was not prepared for such an alternative. I requested three days to consider. At the end of that time I told him I had made up my mind, and would submit to the operations. Accordingly he amputated one of them on the fifteenth of March, and the other on the seventeenth of

April following. Unfortunately for me he cut them off below the ankle joint, from a wish to take as little away as possible; the sores extended above the place, and have never completely healed. By the month of August I could creep about on my hands and knees.

My case excited great compassion, and a subscription was raised for me by Governor Baranoff and the officers of the ships that lay in the harbour, which amounted to one hundred and eighty rubles.

Whilst in the hospital, the brig arrived that had been despatched to Sannack for the goods saved from the wreck. With her came Mr. Bander, and also the mate and boatswain of the Eclipse, who had left Captain O'Cain in consequence of a difference that had taken place. They informed me that he had nearly completed the vessel, which was a brig of about seventy tons, and that he would find no difficulty in manning her with Russians and Indians. I afterwards heard from some Indians, who had come with despatches from Oonalaska, that the vessel was launched, and had sailed from Sannack. What became of her afterwards, I never could learn with certainty, but it was reported that she had foundered at sea, and all on board perished.

The mate, second mate, and boatswain, left Kodiak in a ship called the Neva, bound for Sitcha, an island near Norfolk Sound, where the Russians have lately established a settlement, from whence, I understand, they went to China in an American ship.

Mr. Baranoff, the governor, went to Sitcha at the same time, leaving Mr. Bander in charge of the colony.

When I had tolerably recovered my strength, I was employed by that gentleman in teaching eight Indian children the English language, in order that they might be qualified to act as interpreters to the American ships that frequently touch at these islands. My pupils were between the ages of eight and thirteen, and had all been taught the Russian language, of which, by this time, I understood a little.

I had to labour under great difficulties for want of books and grammars, and was obliged to form the letters of the alphabet in the best manner I was able. This was no easy task to me, both from want of practice, and the state of my right hand, which I could with difficulty open or shut. I however succeeded in teaching them to read the letters, but my farther progress was interrupted by my departure from the island. I have very little doubt of my ultimate success, had I remained, for the boys were uncommonly quick and apt to learn.

The island of Kodiak is the principal possession of the Russians on the northwest coast of America. It is above a hundred miles long, from northeast to southwest, and about fifty across at the wider part; but its breadth is very irregular, the shore being indented with deep bays and inlets.

The climate is by no means favourable; the snow lies on the ground till the end of April, and although the cold in winter is not very intense, the season is seldom free from fogs, snow, or rain. The summers are also very wet, and subject to frequent fogs.

Kodiak contains but a scanty population, the inhabitants are scattered through eight or ten villages upon the coast, and are employed in collecting furs for the Russian American Company. These villages, in general, consist of a few Indian families, who are under the charge of a Russian overseer.

No part of the island is cultivated, except a garden or two near the town, and a little barley at the village of Superscoff. It contains, however, a great deal of fine timber, chiefly larches, spruces, and other kinds of pine. Many of the trees are large enough to make spars of considerable dimensions.

Alexandria,* the principal town on the island, and the residence of the governor, is situated on the eastern side of an extensive bay. It possesses an excellent harbour, being well sheltered by several small islands that lie to the southwest. The eastern entrance, which is the safest, is not above a mile wide, and is defended by a battery or small fort. There is also an entrance to the west; but it is narrow and intricate, and requires a leading wind to pass through.

The town consists of about fifty houses, built of logs, the seams of which are calked with moss, and the roofs thatched with grass; they are, in general, divided into three apartments

* This place is named St. Paul by Captain Lisianski. We must suppose that since his visit in 1803, the name has been changed in honour of the present Emperor. Dr. Langsdorf merely calls it the new harbour of Kodiak.

below, and as many on the upper story. They are heated by stoves or ovens; when the wood is reduced to ashes, the vent is closed by means of a slide fitted for the purpose, and the heated air then diffusing itself through the room, renders it extremely comfortable. The windows, instead of being glazed, are covered with pieces of the gut of the seal, split up and sewed together; this, after being well oiled, is stretched on a frame, and defended from the wind by cross-bars on each side. Talc is also used for the same purpose. This substance is found in flakes about the size of the palm of the hand, and several of these are puttied together to form a pane.

About sixty Indians reside at this place; they live in a large circulur building or barrack, called the Cazerne Aleuskoi.

The town also possesses a church, a barrack for the Russian convicts, a school, and several storehouses belonging to the N. W. Company.

At the school the children of the natives are taught the Russian language, writing, and arithmetic; there were about fifty scholars, and as far as I could judge, from the few under my charge, there is no difficulty in teaching them these acquirements.

Here, as at Kamschatka, most of the Russians are married to native women.

This is the principal depot of the American Company;* the furs collected at the different settlements on the coast are sent here, and lodged in the Company's stores till ships arrive to carry them to Kamschatka, whence they are sent to China, or overland to St. Petersburgh.

The natives, in return for the furs which they procure for the Company, receive cloth, powder and shot, beads, toys, and articles of luxury, such as rum, tobacco, and snuff, of which they are immoderately fond.

A considerable trade is carried on with the Americans who call at these islands. Their ships take on board a certain number of natives, with their baidarkas, and implements of fishing and hunting. They then proceed to the coast of California, where there is great abundance of fur seals, and otters, and with

* This Company was established in the reign of the Empress Catharine II. for the purpose of giving solidity and effect to the fur trade; and the better to promote these purposes, all the islands lying between Kamschatka and the Russian part of the northwest coast of America, were granted them in perpetuity. His present majesty, Alexander I. has extended the privileges of the Company, and graciously declared himself their immediate patron.

Lisianski, p. 13.

the assistance of the Indians, generally complete their cargoes in two seasons. On their return the American Company are entitled to a certain proportion of their furs, as an equivalent for the labour of the Indians. The Eclipse was on a voyage of this description, when chartered by the Russians to bring a cargo from China.

A few miles to the west of Alexandria, there is another village called Superscoff, the property of a Russian of that name, who had been settled there above fifteen years. From this place the town of Alexandria derives its principal supply of salmon and dried fish.—They had a herd of black cattle consisting of seventy, all sprung from one cow which Superscoff brought with him. The milk, butter, and cheese, used at the town, were brought from this place.

Their stock of cattle, having been but recently introduced, is too small to admit of their slaughtering any, and bear's flesh is the only fresh meat consumed upon the island. The bears are either shot or caught in traps; the trap is merely a piece of board, about two inches thick, and two feet square, stuck full of spikes, barbed, and kept extremely sharp; this is set in their paths, and covered with dust; from the weight of the animal, when he sets down his foot, the spikes enter it; to assist himself in pulling the first away, he plants another on the trap, and continues his exertions, till, at last, all his four feet are transfixed, when he falls on his back, and is taken.

The natives of the Fox islands, or Aleuskoi, as they are called by the Russians, are low in stature, broad in the visage, with dark eyes and hair.

The principal article of their dress is a large frock called a parka, made of fur or skin, frequently of the skins of sea-fowls, which they wear with the feathers out during the day, and next their skin at night. This piece of dress is nearly the same in both sexes. When at sea, they wear a frock of another kind, called a camelengka, made of the gut of the seal, to which a hood is attached, and tied close round the face, the sleeves being equally tight at the wrist. Upon their limbs they frequently wear boots and breeches in one piece, made of seal hide, over which the camelengka is fastened close, so that their dress is perfectly water-proof.

They are extremely fond of ornaments, particularly beads, with which the women decorate themselves in great profusion, sewing them round the neck, skirts, and wrists of their skin frocks. They also wear them in their ears, or suspend them from a hole made in their under lip, and sometimes hang them round each end of a bone about five inches long, which they pass through the gristle of the nose, called by sailors their spritsail-yard. They do not tattoo themselves like the Sandwich islanders, but they often paint or rather daub their faces in streaks, with red ochre and train oil.

Their canoes are made of the skin of sea-lions, stretched over slight wooden frames; Those of the largest size, called baiderais, are open, and can contain sixty or seventy people; the smaller kind, called baidarkas, being quite close, have a hole in the covering, or deck, for each sitter, and carry one, two, or three persons. They are rowed either with double-bladed paddles, which are held by the middle, or by single-bladed ones, with crutch handles, which are shifted to each side alternately; the rowers sit with their faces to the bow, and pull them with great swiftness. It is wonderful what long voyages they make in these slight boats; several of them came from Oonalaska to Kodiak during my stay in that island. No water can get into them in the roughest weather, for the camelengka, a gut frock, which Indians wear when at sea, is stuffed tight round them at the hole. From their flat construction, and extreme lightness, the weight of the people sitting in these canoes, renders them top heavy, and many accidents arise from their oversetting. In this respect, the single-holed ones are much the safest, for even when overset, a slight exertion is sufficient to right them.

In catching seals, and other amphibious animals, these people show great dexterity and ingenuity. Concealing themselves behind rocks, they decoy them by throwing a seal skin, blown out like a bladder, into the sea. To this is fixed a line made of the sinew of the whale, by which they draw it to them, when it is followed by the seals, who take it for an animal of their own species. As soon as within reach, they are killed with spears, or bows and arrows.

The natives, as I have already observed, are converts to the Greek church, but their religion consists in little more than crossing themselves, whenever they enter a house; they are however, abundantly superstitious, and put complete faith in the predictions of their shamans, or astrologers. Whilst I was there an eclipse of the moon took place, on which occasion they confidently affirmed that it was the sign of great events happening in Europe. Indeed, not only the natives, but the Russians themselves seemed to be of the same opinion; and the next ship bringing intelligence of war between England and Russia, served to confirm their belief.

The food of the natives consists of fish, fresh or dried, principally salmon; blubber, or whale fat; whale and seal oil; the flesh of seals and other amphibious animals; and berries preserved in oil.

In consequence of this diet, as well as the state of filth in which they live, they are very liable to the scurvy; indeed, few of them are free from ulcers and scorbutic eruptions.

On the return of the Neva from Sitcha, she was ordered to be prepared for a voyage to the Sandwich Islands, and was provided with a supply of adzes, hatchets, teeth of the sea-horse, and other articles suited for that market.

It would appear that the Russians had determined to form a settlement upon these islands; at least, preparations were made for that purpose; and I was informed by the commandant, that if I chose, I might get a situation as interpreter. The ship had a house in frame on board, and intimation was given that volunteers would be received; none, however, offered; and I never observed that any other steps were taken in this affair.

Being sure of meeting with American vessels at the Sandwich Islands, in which I might get to Europe or America, I expressed a desire to embrace this opportunity of quitting Kodiak, and was accordingly permitted to take my passage in the ship.

The Neva had a crew of seventy-five seamen, belonging to the Russian imperial service, and was commanded by captain Hageimeister, who had been bred in the British navy, and could speak English fluently. The ship herself was British built, and had made a voyage round the world.*

* This ship sailed round the world in the Russian expedition under captain Krusenstern, and was commanded by captain Lisianski, who has published an account of the voyage. He talks in raptures of her good qualities. " As to the Neva itself, I shall be excused if,

The preparations for the expedition being completed, we left the harbour on the 11th of December, O. S. with a fair wind, and soon lost sight of the island.

with the warmth of a sailor, I declare, that there never sailed a more lovely vessel, or one more complete and perfect in all its parts. So little had it suffered from the length of the voyage, and even from the disaster of striking on the coral rocks at our newly discovered island, that, in a few weeks, ts was again ready for sea, and was despatched to the north west coast of America.

Lisianski's Voyage, p. 317

CHAPTER VIII.

Voyage to Sandwich Islands—Make Owhyhee—Touch at Mowee—Proceed to Wahoo—Tamaahmaah and other chiefs come on board—Author resides three months with the King—Account of his mode of life—Remove to the house of Isaac Davis—Account of him—Death of Terremytee, the King's brother, and transactions that took place on that occasion—Remarkable water-spout—Author receives a grant of land from the King, to which he removes—Residence there—Arrival of the ship Duke of Portland—Anecdotes of the King—Departure from the Sandwich Islands.

We proceeded on our voyage to the Sandwich Islands, and enjoyed fine weather, with favourable winds.

No land was seen from the time we quitted the Fox Islands, till the 27th of January.

On that morning, at day break, we discovered the mountains of Owhyhee, at the distance of ten leagues. In the afternoon, we were close in with the land, and coasted along the north side of the island.

The breeze being light, several canoes came from the shore with fresh provisions. We stood off and on for some time, carrying on a brisk trade with the natives; amongst other things supplied by them, we were surprised to find sheep and goats, the breed of which, although but recently introduced, has increased so rapidly that they already form an article of trade.

We passed the foot of Mouna-kaa,* one of the highest mountains in the world. The sides are extremely steep, and although situated within the tropics, the summit is perpetually covered with snow; a narrow tract of level ground lies between the base of the mountain and the sea, terminating in high abrupt clifts; presenting at a distance a most barren appearance. On a nearer approach, however, we could observe numerous patches of cultivated land, and the lower parts of the mountain covered with wood. Farther to the west, the plains are of greater extent, the country well wooded, and in a high state of cultivation; with many villages and houses,

* Captain King estimates the height of this mountain at not less than 18,400 feet; exceeding the peak of Teneriffe, according to the computation of the Chevalier Borda, by nearly 6,000 feet. The result of a trigonometrical measurement by the latter, gives 1,742 toises, as the altitude of that mountan above the level of the sea. *Vide Cook's Third Voyage*, vol iii. p. 103. and *Voyage fait par ordre du Roi, an* 1771—2, tom. i. p 119.

presenting every appearance of a numerous and industrious population.

Mouna-roa,* one of the mountains in the interior, is a volcano; a few years before this time a violent eruption took place, when it sent forth a stream of lava which ran into the sea. Isaac Davis, with whom I afterwards resided, and who had gone in a canoe to witness it, informed me that where the lava joined the sea, the heat was so intense that he could not approach nearer than fifty yards. We did not see any flame or smoke isssuing from the crater.

We made sail in the evening, and reached Mowee the following day.

Whilst running along the southeast side of the island, several canoes came off with refreshments. In one of them was a white man, calling himself Joseph Wynn, an American. He had resided several years upon the island, where he had a family, and cultivated a piece of land, which had been granted to him by Crymakoo, a powerful chief.

I afterwards learned that his real name was Angus Maccallum, a native of Houstoun, in

* According to the admeasurement of Dr Horner, astronomer to the Russian expedition under captain Krusenstern, in 1804, the height of of Mouna-roa is 2,254 toises. *Krusenstern's Voyage*, vol. 1. p. 193.

Renfrewshire. Having served with his brother in the Diana frigate, and coming from the same part of the country, a great degree of intimacy naturally took place between us, and we had much conversation together.

Amongst other things, I told him that I understood the Russians had some intention of forming a settlement on the Sandwich islands. This reached the captain's ears; and he gave me a severe reprimand, for having, as he expressed it, betrayed their secrets. He desired me to say no more on the subject in future, otherwise I should not be permitted to quit the ship.

I know not what obstacle prevented this plan from being carried into effect; but although the Neva remained several months in the country, I never heard any more of the settlement.

We came to anchor in the harbour of Lahina. The captain went ashore and returned with a supply of fresh provisions. I wished much to have accompanied him, but the surf rendered the landing too difficult for one in my helpless condition.

Tamaahmaah, king of Owhyhee, Mowee, Wahoo, and the adjoining islands, resided some years at this place. His house, which we could distinctly see from the ship, was built of brick, after the European manner. Of late, he has fixed his residence at Wahoo; upon learning of which, the captain determined to proceed thither.

The island of Mowee is of great height. At a distance it appears like two islands; a low flat piece of land running completely across, and dividing it into two peninsulas. Maccallum informed me that it was very fertile; that provisions were abundant, and much cheaper than at either Owhyhee or Wahoo.

We weighed on the morning of the 29th, and passing between the islands of Morokai and Ranai, reached the harbour of Hanaroora, on the south side of Wahoo, the same evening.

A number of natives came off, as usual, the moment the ship hove in sight. King Tamaahmaah was in a large double canoe; on his coming along side, he sent his interpreter on board to announce his arrival.

The captain immediately went to the gangway to receive his majesty, and shook hands with him when he came upon deck.

He was, on this occasion, dressed as a European, in a blue coat and gray pantaloons.

Immediately on his coming aboard, the king entered into earnest conversation with the captain. Amongst other questions, he asked whether the ship was English or American? being informed that she was Russian, he answered, "Meitei, meitei," or, very good. A handsome scarlet cloak, edged and ornamented with ermine, was presented to him from the governor of the Aleutian islands. After trying it on, he gave it to his attendants to be taken on shore. I never saw him use it afterwards. In other canoes came Tamena, one of his queens, Crymakoo, his brother-in-law, and other chiefs of inferior rank.

My appearance attracted the notice, and excited the compassion of the queen; and finding it was my intention to remain upon the islands, she invited me to take up my residence in her house. I gladly availed myself of this offer, at which she expressed much pleasure; it being a great object of ambition amongst the higher ranks to have white people to reside with them. When the ship was brought to anchor, she sent me ashore in one of her canoes.

Captain Hagemeister recommended me at the same time to the notice of the king, by informing him, that I could not only make and repair the sails of his vessels, but also weave the cloth of which they were made.

The king assured him that I should be treated with the utmost kindness. It will be seen in the sequel how well he performed his promise.

Upon landing I was much struck with the beauty and fertility of the country, so different from the barrenness of the Fox islands. The village of Hanaroora, which consisted of several hundred houses, is well shaded with large cocoa-nut trees. The king's residence, built close upon the shore, and surrounded by a pallisade upon the land side, was distinguished by the British colours and a battery of sixteen carriage guns, belonging to his ship, the Lily Bird, which at this time lay unrigged in the harbour. This palace consisted merely of a range of huts, viz. the king's eating-house, his sleeping-house, the queen's house, a store, powder-magazine, and guard-house, with a few huts for the attendants, all constructed after the fashion of the country.

At a short distance were two extensive store-houses, built of stone, which contained the European articles belonging to the king.

I was conducted to the house occupied by the two queens. It consisted of one large apartment, spread with mats; at one end of which the attendants of both sexes slept, and at the other the queens occasionally slept when the king was in the morai.

They and their attendants always eat here, and Tamena wished me to join them; but as I had been informed by Crymakoo, that if I did so, I should not be allowed to eat with men, I resolved to decline her offer.

The Neva remained in the harbour three months, during which time I ate my victuals on board. At the end of that period, having completed a cargo of provisions, consisting of salted pork and dried taro root, she sailed for Kodiak and Kamschatka. I was then invited by the king to take my meals in his eating-house, and at the same time he desired a young American, of the name of William Moxely, a native of Norfolk in Virginia, who understood the language, to eat along with me, to act as my interpreter. The king's mode of life was very simple; he breakfasted at eight, dined at noon, and supped at sunset.

His principal chiefs being always about his person, there were generally twenty or thirty persons present; after being seated upon mats spread on the floor, at dinner a dish of poe, or taro pudding, was set before each of them, which they ate with their fingers instead of spoons. This fare, with salt fish and consecrated pork from the morai, formed the whole of the repast, no other food being permitted in the king's house. A plate, knife and fork, with boiled potatoes, were, however, always set down before Moxely and me, by his majesty's orders. He concluded his meal by drinking half a glass of rum; but the bottle was immediately sent away, the liquor being tabooed, or interdicted to his guests. The breakfast and supper consisted of fish and sweet potatoes.

The respect paid to the king's person, to his house, and even to his food, formed a remarkable contrast to the simplicity of his mode of living.

Whenever he passed, his subjects were obliged to uncover their heads and shoulders. The same ceremony took place upon their entering, or even passing his residence; and every house which he entered was ever after honoured with the same marks of respect. Once, when employed in the house of Isaac Davis, making a loom for the king, I observed him passing, and being ignorant of this custom, requested him to enter and observe my progress; but he declined doing so, informing me of the consequence. He, therefore, seated himself at the door, till I brought out my work for his inspection.

When his food was carrying from the cooking-house, every person within hearing of the call Noho, or, sit down, given by the bearers, was obliged to uncover himself, and squat down on his hams.*

This ceremony was particularly inconvenient when the water used in the king's house was carried past; there being none of a good quality near Hanaroora, it was necessary to bring it from the mountains, a distance of five miles. The calabash carriers were obliged, when any person appeared in sight, to call out Noho. They, however, ran past as quick as

* Scotice, "on his *hunkers.*" The emphatic word used by the author in describing this particular mode of genuflexion, and which has no English synonyme into which it can be translated, is thus defined by Jamieson: "to sit with the hips hanging downwards, and the weight of the body depending on the knees."—*Scot. Dict. verb Hunkers.*

"Wi' ghastly e'e, poor Tweedle-dee,
Upon his *hunkers* bended."—BURNS.

they could, not to detain his majesty's subjects in so unpleasant an attitude.

White people were not required to pay these honors, though scrupulously exacted from the natives.

Tamaahmaah was most attentive in performing the duties of religion, and constantly attended the morai on the taboo days, which took place about four times each month. The ceremonies lasted one day and two nights; during which time no person was permitted to pass the bounds of the morai.

When the king was absent on these occasions, I did not experience the same attention as at other times; the attendants became very remiss in providing my dinner, and I was sometimes obliged to go without it altogether.

I accompanied the king once to the morai; but not relishing the confinement, and being unwilling to make complaints, I removed, about the beginning of May, to the house of Isaac Davis, a Welshman, who had been about twenty years upon the island, and remained with him till the king gave me a grant of land about six months afterwards.

Mr. Davis arrived at the Sandwich islands as mate of a small American schooner. The captain, a very young man, having incautiously permitted the natives to go on board, without any restriction, a chief, of the name of Tamahmotoo, observing this, planned her capture. For which purpose a number of natives, under various pretences, crowded into the vessel, and, upon a signal being given, threw the whole crew, five in number, into the sea. Davis, being an excellent swimmer, laid hold of one of the canoes, from which, however, he was beat off by paddles. He swam to another, where the natives also attempted to beat him off; but being a stout, athletic man, he was able to keep his hold. Having no arms, they attempted to put him to death, by holding him under the water, and beating him with their paddles; and also endeavoured to strangle him, by placing his neck across one of the beams of the canoe, and trampling upon him. But by this time the rest of the crew having been destroyed, and the schooner taken possession of, they relented, and ceased to torment him any farther. He was carried ashore blind, and almost lifeless, and it was eighteen months before he recovered his sight. He told me, that, before this time, he had never believed in the existence of a God, and had led a very sinful life; that, upon the near prospect of death, the idea of his offences filled him with terror; and that he tried to repeat the Lord's Prayer, and felt himself strengthened after doing so.

Tamaahmaah, who was at a distant part of the island, was extremely indignant at Tamahmotoo when he heard of this outrage.

He took the vessel from him for the purpose of restoring her to her owners, and showed the utmost kindness to Davis. Nearly at the same time another Englishman, of the name of Young, was detained upon the island.

These two constantly attached themselves to Tamaahmaah; and, from their knowledge of fire-arms, proved of essential service in the expeditions in which he conquered Mowee, Morotoi, and Wahoo.

They were rewarded, by being raised to the rank of chiefs, and received extensive grants of land.

When Tamaahmaah removed to Wahoo, Davis accompanied him, and he left Young as governor of Owhyhee. These two he always treated with greater confidence than any of the native chiefs. Davis had extensive grants of land on several of the islands. Upon Wahoo alone he had estates on which were four or five hundred people, who cultivated the land, and paid him a rent in kind. These were exempted from the taxes paid by the other chiefs for their lands; but Davis frequently made the king presents of feather cloaks, and other valuable articles.

He was married to a native woman, by whom he had no children. By a former wife he had three, two of whom were left under the charge of Mr. Young of Owhyhee. His house was distinguished from those of the natives only by the addition of a shed in front to keep off the sun; within, it was spread with mats, but had no furniture, except two benches to sit upon. He lived very much like the natives, and had acquired such a taste for poe, that he preferred it to any other food. We had, however, at all times abundance of pork, goat's flesh, and mutton, and frequently beef sent by Young from Owhyhee; and in the mornings and evenings we had tea. His wealth, consisting of mats, feathers, and cloth, the produce of the island, and a large assortment of European articles, which he had acquired by trading with the ships that touched here; these were contained in a large storehouse, built of stone, adjoining his dwelling.

My first employment was to overhaul the sails of the king's vessels, and to repair such as were out of order. After working two or three months at this, he desired me to make some canvass.

Having informed him that a loom was necessary, he ordered Boyd, his principal carpenter, to make one. This, however, Boyd declined, from an illiberal notion held by many of the white people, that the natives should be taught nothing that would render them independent of strangers. He told the king he did not know how to make looms; upon which I undertook to make one myself; although, by so doing, I incurred the displeasure of many of my countrymen. Davis had a native servant called Jack, who worked as a Tailor, and was a very handy fellow. This man showed much anxiety to observe how I proceeded; but his master told me by no means to allow him, as he was so quick he would soon learn to make a loom himself. When I said I had no wish to make it a secret, he replied, that if the natives could weave cloth, and supply themselves, ships would have no encouragement to call at the islands. Another instance of this narrow way of thinking occurred, when a brother of the queen's, whose name I do not remember, but who was usually called by the white people, John Adams, wished me to teach him to read, Davis would not permit me, observing, "they will soon know more than ourselves."

The making of the loom, from want of assistance, and want of practice, proved a very tedious job. I succeeded tolerably well at last; and having procured a supply of thread, spun by the women from the fibres of the plant of which their fishing lines are made, I began my operations.* After working a small piece, I took it to the king as a specimen. He approved of it in every respect except breadth, which was only about half a yard, saying, he wished it made wide enough for an awning to a ship. This was beyond my power; but I told him I could make it a yard wide, and then sow it up into any size. He accordingly ordered me to make a loom of the necessary dimensions.—The small piece I wove he kept, and showed it to every captain that arrived as a specimen of

* The author was obliged to employ a boy to work the treadles not being able to work them himself from the loss of his feet.

the manufacture of the country. I had nearly finished the other loom, when the ship arrived in which I quitted the island.

During the time I resided with Davis, Terremytee, the king's brother, died. His body lay in state for a few days, in the morai; and was afterwards buried, according to custom, in a secret manner.

The public mourning that took place on this occasion was of so extraordinary a nature, that, had I not been an eye-witness, I could not have given credit to it.

The natives cut off their hair, and went about completely naked. Many of them, particularly the women, disfigured themselves by knocking out their front teeth, and branding their faces with red hot stones, and the small end of calabashes, which they held burning to their faces till a circular mark was produced; whilst, at the same time, a general, I believe I may say an universal, public prostitution of the women took place; the queens and the widow of the deceased alone exempted.

When the captain of a ship that lay in the harbour remonstrated with the king upon these disgraceful scenes, he answered that such was the law, and he could not prevent them.

About this time an immense water-spout broke in the harbour. It was first observed in the south, about noon. The day was fine, with a clear atmosphere, and nearly calm. When I saw it first, it appeared about the thickness of a ship's mast, reaching from the sea to a heavy dark cloud that hung immediately over it. It approached slowly, the cloud gradually increasing in size. When it came near, we could observe the water ascending in a spiral direction, and the sea round its base boiling up in great agitation. At this time it seemed about the thickness of a hogshead. The tide was fortunately out; and upon crossing the reef, about an hour after its first appearance, the column broke, and such a mass of water fell, that the sea in the harbour was raised at least three feet upon the beach. No squall was experienced, nor did any rain fall. Hundreds of dead fish were picked up upon the reef, and along shore after it broke. I have seen several water-spouts at sea, and one that was nearly on board the ship in which I was, but none of them at all equal in magnitude to this.

The natives quitted their houses, and fled with the utmost precipitation in a direction opposite to that in which it approached. I was informed, that a few years before, one had broken on the north side of the island, by which a number of houses were washed away and many people drowned.

In the month of November the king was pleased to grant me about sixty acres of land, situated upon the Wymummee, or Pearl-water, an inlet of the sea about twelve miles to the west of Hanaroora. I immediately removed thither; and it being Macaheite time, during which canoes are tabooed, I was carried on men's shoulders. We passed by footpaths, winding through an extensive and fertile plain, the whole of which is in the highest state of cultivation. Every stream was carefully embanked, to supply water for the taro beds. Where there was no water, the land was under crops of yams and sweet potatoes. The roads and numerous houses are shaded by cocoa-nut trees, and the sides of the mountains covered with wood to a great height. We halted two or three times, and were treated by the natives with the utmost hospitality. My farm, called Wymannoo, was upon the east side of the river, four or five miles from its mouth. Fifteen people, with their families, resided upon it, who cultivated the ground as my servants. There were three houses upon the property: but I found it most agreeable to live with one of my neighbours, and get what I wanted from my own land. This person's name was William Stevenson, a native of Borrowstounness. He had been a convict, and escaped from New South Wales; but was, notwithstanding, an industrious man, and conducted himself in general with great propriety. He had married a native, and had a family of several children.—He was the first who introduced into the island the mode of distilling a spirit from the tee-root, of which, however, he became so fond, that the king was obliged to deprive him of his still. When I knew him he had bound himself by an oath, not to taste spirits except at the new year, at which time he indulged to the greatest excess. He chiefly employed himself in his garden, and had a large stock of European vegetables.

In the end of February, I heard there was a ship at Hanaroora, and went up with a canoe-load of provisions, wishing to provide myself with some clothes, and, if possible, a few books. She proved to be the Duke of Portland, South-sea whaler, bound for England. When I learned this, I felt the wish to see my native country and friends once more so strong, that I could not resist the opportunity that now offered. In addition to these motives, the state of my feet had of late given me considerable uneasiness; the sores had never healed, and I was anxious for medical assistance, in the hopes of having a cure performed. I was, indeed, leaving a situation of ease, and comparative affluence, for one where, labouring under the disadvantage of the loss of my feet, I knew I must earn a scanty subsistence. I was a tolerable sail-maker; and I knew, that if my sores healed, I could gain a comfortable livelihood at that employment. These hopes were never realized; the state of my limbs renders me quite unable to hold a bolt-rope, and necessity has compelled me to betake myself to a more precarious and less agreeable occupation.

The king was on board the ship at the time, and I asked his permission to take my passage home. He inquired my reason for wishing to quit the island, and whether I had any cause of complaint. I told him I had none; that I was sensible I was much better here than I could be any where else, but that I was desirous to see my friends once more. He said, if his belly told him to go, he would do it; and that if mine told me so, I was at liberty.

He then desired me to give his compliments to King George. I told him that, though born in his dominions, I had never seen King George; and that, even in the city where he lived, there were thousands who had never seen him. He expressed much surprise at this, and asked if he did not go about among his people, to learn their wants, as he did? I answered, that he did not do it himself, but that he had men who did it for him. Tamaahmaah shook his head at this, and said, that other people could never do it so well as he could himself.

He sent a handsome cloak of feathers by Captain Spence as a present to his majesty, accompanied by a letter, which I heard him dictate to the captain. The purport of it was to remind him of Captain Vancouver's promise, that a man of war, armed with brass guns, and loaded with European articles, should be sent to him; and added, that he was sorry he was so far away that he could not help him in his wars; and concluded, by requesting his acceptance of the cloak as a proof of his regard

Having procured the king's permission to depart, I went on shore to take leave of my friends; particularly Isaac Davis, and my patroness, the queen, who had always treated me with the utmost kindness. On this occasion she presented me with several valuable mats to sleep upon on board the ship.

It will be believed that I did not leave Wahoo without the deepest regret. I had now been thirteen months upon the island; during which time I had experienced nothing but kindness and friendship from all ranks—from my much honoured master, the king, down to the lowest native. A crowd of people attended me to the boat; unaccustomed to conceal their feelings, they expressed them with great vehemence; and I heard the lamentations of my friends on shore long after I had reached the ship.

We sailed next day, being the 4th of March.

CHAPTER IX.

Description of Wahoo—Extent—Whyteete-bay—Account of Tamaahmaah's navy—Town and harbour of Hanaroora—Bass's harbour—Wymumme, or Pearl-river—State of cultivation—Breed of cattle—Account of the white people resident on the island.

THE island of Wahoo lies about seven leagues to the northwest of Morotai, and about thirty from Owhyhee, in the same direction; it is nearly forty miles in length from northwest to southeast, and almost half that extent in breadth.

Although only of secondary size, it has become the most important island in the groupe, both on account of its superior fertility, and because it possesses the only secure harbour to be met with in the Sandwich islands.

In consequence of this, and of the facility with which fresh provisions can be procured, almost every vessel* that navigates the north

* During the thirteen months the author remained on the island, there were at least twelve ships called at Wahoo, of which two were English, the Duke of Portland, captain Spence; and the

Pacific puts in here to refit. This is probably the principal reason why the king has chosen it as his place of residence; perhaps the vicinity to Atooi and Onehow, the only islands independent of himself, and the conquest of which he is said to meditate, is another and no less powerful motive.

The south coast of the island extends from Diamond-hill on the east, to Barber's Point* on the west, a distance of about twenty-four miles. A range of mountains run almost parallel to the shore, from which it is separated by a fertile plain, which varies in breadth; at Hanaroora, where it is broadest, the distance from the sea to the mountains is about five miles.

A reef of coral runs along the whole extent of this shore, within a quarter of a mile of the land; the greater part of it dries at low water, and in the inside it is in many places

Otter, Jobelin. One Russian, the Neva; and the remainder Americans, viz. the Catherine, Blanchard; O'Kean, Winship; Otter, Hill; Vancouver, Swift; Liddy, Brown; Dromo, Woodward; and three or four more, when he was at Pearl river, whose names he does not remember.

* Captain Portlocke distinguishes the first of these points by the name of Point Dick, and the latter by that of Point Banks.

Portlocke, p. 75.

too shallow even for canoes, except at full tide.*

Whyteete bay, where captain Vancouver anchored, is formed by the land falling back from the southern promontory of the island, called by the white people Diamond-hill. It is open to the south one half of the compass, and there being no channel, ships are obliged to anchor on the outside of the reef.

Tamaahmaah formerly resided at this place, and great part of his navy were hauled up on the shore round the bay. I counted more than thirty vessels; they are kept with the utmost care, having sheds built over them, their spars laid alongside, and their rigging and cables preserved in stores.

They are chiefly sloops and schooners, under forty tons burden, and have all been built by his own carpenters, principally na-

* Captain Broughton mentions a harbour which he surveyed, called Fair Haven, which lies five or six miles E. S. E. of Whyteete; it is formed by an opening through the reefs, with a clear channel, in a N. N. E. direction. The wind generally blows fresh out of it, rendering it necessary to warp in, as there is no room for working. The harbour, though of small extent, is ssfe and convenient, with five fathoms sandy bottom within the spits. A fine stream of fresh water empties itself at the head Ii was discovered in 1794 by Mr. Brown, master of the Butterworth, the same who was afterwards murdered by the natives at this place. *Vide Broughton's Voyage*, p. 39.

tives, under the direction of an Englishman of the name of Boyd.

He possesses one ship of about two hundred tons, called the Lily Bird. This vessel was originally an American, which arrived from the coast of California in a leaky condition. He purchased her from the captain, by giving his largest schooner in exchange, and paying the difference in dollars. She was repaired by his own carpenters, and laid up at Hanaroora, along side a wharf built for the purpose. The remainder of his fleet, ten or twelve more, were hauled up at the same place, except one small sloop, which he kept as a packet between Wahoo and Owhyhee. She was navigated by native seamen, under the command of an Englishman, of the name of Clerk, who had formerly been mate of the Lily Bird.

Three miles to the west of Whyteete is the town of Hanaroora, now the capital of the island, and residence of the king. The harbour is formed by the reef, which shelters it from the sea, and ships can ride within in safety in any weather, upon a fine sandy bottom. There is a good channel through the reef, with three or four fathoms water;

but if there is a swell it is not easily discovered, as the sea often breaks completely across. Pilots, however, are always to be had; John Hairbottle, captain of the Lily Bird, generally acted as such. The best anchorage is in five fathoms water, about two cables length from the shore, directly in front of the village. Ships sometimes anchor on the outside of the reef, but they run the risk of having their cables cut by the coral.

The entrance to this harbour may probably, at no very distant period, be filled up by the growth of the coral, which must be rapid indeed, if Hairbottle, the pilot, was correct, when he informed me that he knew a difference of three feet during the time he had been at Hanaroora.*

A small river runs by the back of the village, and joins the sea at the west side of the harbour; owing to the flatness of the country, the water is brackish, and there is none fresh to be had within several miles of the place. Ships, however, can be supplied at

* Hairbottle had been fifteen years on the island, he was mate of the Jackall, which arrived about the end of 1794. *Vide Broughton.*

a moderate rate by the natives, who bring it from the spring in calabashes.

Six miles to the westward is Bass's harbour, also formed by an entrance through the reef; within it is well sheltered, with good anchorage in five or six fathoms; but there being no village in the vicinity, it is little frequented.*

Wymumme, or Pearl river, lies about seven miles farther to the westward. This inlet extends ten or twelve miles up the country. The entrance is not more than a quarter of a mile wide, and is only navigable for small craft; the depth of water on the bar, at the highest tides, not exceeding seven feet; farther up it is nearly two miles across. There is an ilse in it, belonging to Manina, the king's interpreter, in which he keeps a numerous flock of sheep and goats.

* This inlet is evidently the same which Captain Vancouver surveyed, and which, he says, is named Oporoah; finding that, in consequence of the bar, it was only navigable for small craft, the survey was not continued. He merely says, that within "it seemed to spread out, and to terminate in two bays about a mile farther to the northward" He mentions another opening to the eastward, called by the natives Honoonoona, which must be either Bass's harbour or Hanaroora. From the similarity of the name, it is more probably the latter place; but he passed it without examination, being informed that it was shallower than the other inlet.

Pearls and mother-of-pearl shells are found here in considerable quantity. Since the king has learned their value, he has kept the fishing to himself, and employs divers for the purpose.

Ten miles to the west of this is Barber's Point, (so called from the captain of a ship wrecked there,) the northwest extremity of the island. It is very low, and extends a considerable way into the sea.

The tides upon this coast do not rise more than four feet at springs; it is high water about three at full and change of the moon. The force of the current is scarcely perceptible.

The flat land along shore is highly cultivated; taro root, yams, and sweet potatoes, are the most common crops; but taro forms the chief object of their husbandry, being the principal article of food amongst every class of inhabitants.

The mode of culture is extremely laborious, as it is necessary to have the whole field laid under water; it is raised in small patches, which are seldom above a hundred yards square; these are surrounded by embankments, generally about six feet high, the sides of which are planted with sugar-canes, with a walk at top; the fields are intersected by drains or acqueducts, constructed with great labour and ingenuity, for the purpose of supplying the water necessary to cover them.

The ground is first carefully dug and levelled with a wooden spade, called maiai, which the labourers use, squatting on their hams and heels. After this, it is firmly beat down by treading it with their feet till it is close enough to contain water.

The plants are propagated by planting a small cutting from the upper part of the root with the leaves adhering. The water is then let in, and covers the surface to the depth of twelve or eighteen inches; in about nine months they are ready for taking up; each plant sends forth a number of shoots, or suckers, all around. This mode of culture is particularly laborious, and in all the operations those engaged are almost constantly up to the middle in the mud.

Notwithstanding this, I have often seen the king working hard in a taro patch. I know not whether this was done with a view of setting an example of industry to his subjects.

Such exertion could scarcely be thought necessary amongst these islanders, who are certainly the most industrious people I ever saw.

The potatoe and yam grounds are neatly inclosed by stone walls, about eighteen inches high. In addition to these native productions, Indian corn, and a great variety of garden stuffs have been lately introduced, and are cultivated with success, chiefly by the white peope.

When the islands were discovered, pigs and dogs were the only useful animals they possessed; but Tamaahmaah has paid so much attention to the preservation of the breeds left by Vancouver, and other navigators, that in a short time the stock of horned cattle, horses, sheep, and goats, will be abundant.

At Owhyhee I was informed that there were many hundreds of cattle running wild, and several in a domestic state. The king had introduced the breed into Wahoo; and at the time I was there he had a herd of nine or ten upon the north side of the island.

Sheep and goats are already very numerous. Several individuals had large flocks of them. The queen had one, consisting of about one hundred and fifty; and Manina had several hundreds on the island in Pearl river. —The king had five horses, of which he was very fond, and used frequently to go out on horseback. I was informed there were still more at Owhyhee.

The cattle lately introduced are pastured upon the hills, and those parts of the country not under cultivation, the fences not being sufficient to confine them. The hogs are kept in pens, and fed on taro leaves, sugar canes, and garbage.

The chiefs are the proprietors of the soil, and let the land in small farms to the lower class, who pay them a rent in kind, generally pigs, cloth, or mats, at four terms in the year.

At one time during my stay, there were nearly sixty white people upon Wahoo alone; but the number was constantly varying, and was considerably diminished before my departure. Although the great majority had been left by American vessels, not above one third of them belonged to that nation; the rest were almost all English, and of these six or eight wer convicts, who had made their escape from New South Wales.

Many inducements are held out to sailors to remain here. If they conduct themselves with propriety, they rank as chiefs, and are entitled to all the privileges of the order; at all events, they are certain of being maintained by some of the chiefs, who are always anxious to have white people about them.

The king has a considerable number in his service, chiefly carpenters, joiners, masons, blacksmiths, and bricklayers; these he rewards liberally with grants of land. Some of these people are sober and industrious; but this is far from being their general character; on the contrary, many of them are idle and dissolute, getting drunk whenever an opportunity presents itself. They have introduced distillation into the island; and the evil consequences, both to the natives and whites, are incalculable. It is no uncommon sight to see a party of them broach a small cask of spirits, and sit drinking for days till they see it out.

There are, however, a few exceptions to this. William Davis, a Welshman, who resided with Isaac Davis, used to rise every morning at five, and go to his fields, where he commonly remained till the same hour in the evening. This singularity puzzled the natives not a little; but they accounted for it, by supposing that he had been one of their own countrymen, who had gone to Caheite, or England, after his death, and had now come back to his native land.

There were no missionaries upon the island during the time I remained in it, at which I was often much surprised.

Most of the whites have married native women, by whom they have families; but they pay little attention either to the education or to the religious instruction of their children. I do not recollect having seen any who knew more than the letters of the alphabet.

CHAPTER X.

Account of the natives—Personal appearance—Ranks—Power of the king—Priests--Capital punishments—Mode of detecting theft—Religious belief—Places of worship and ceremonies—Macaheite—Houses—Food—Ava—Spirits distilled from the tee-root—State of the women—Marriages—Dress—Manufactures—Nets and lines—Modes of fishing—Trade—Price of provisions—Amusements—Funeral Rites—Military—Progress in civilization—Account of Tamaahmaah and family.

THE manners and customs of the Sandwich islanders have been repeatedly described by much abler observers; but my long residence has given me opportunities of noticing many things which have escaped others; and to these I shall, as much as possible, confine my remarks.

The natives, although not tall, are stout and robust in their make, particularly those of the higher rank; their complexion is nut-brown, and they are extremely cleanly in their persons. They are distinguished by great ingenuity in all their arts and manufactures, as well as by a most persevering industry.

They are divided into two great classes: the Erees, or chiefs, and the Cannakamowree, or people. The former are the proprietors of the land, the latter are all under the dominion of some chief, for whom they work, or cultivate the ground, and by whom they are supported in old age. They are not, however, slaves, or attached to the soil, but at liberty to change masters when they think proper.

The supreme government is vested in the king, whose power seems to be completely absolute. He is assisted by the principal chiefs, whom he always keeps about his person; many of these have particular departments to attend to; one chief took charge of the household, and appointed the different surveys to be performed by every individual; another, named Coweeowranee, acted as paymaster; his province was to distribute wages and provisions amongst the people in the king's service.

An elderly chief, of the name of Naai, took a general charge of the whole, and was, in fact, prime minister. He was commonly called Billy Pitt by the white people, and was by no means pleased when they addressed him by any other appellation.

The principal duties of the executive were, however, entrusted to the priests; by them the revenues were collected, and the laws enforced. Superstition is the most powerful engine by which the latter purpose is effected; actual punishment being rare. I knew only one instance of capital punishment; which was that of a man who had violated the sanctity of the morai. Having got drunk, he quitted it during taboo time, and entered the house of a woman. He was immediately seized, and carried back to the morai, where his eyes were put out. After remaining two days in this state, he was strangled, and his body exposed before the principal idol.

The method of detecting theft or robbery, affords a singular instance of the power of superstition over their minds. The party who has suffered the loss applies to one of the priests, to whom he presents a pig, and relates his story.

The following ceremony is then performed; the priest begins by rubbing two pieces of green wood upon each other, till, by the friction, a kind of powder, like snuff, is produced, which is so hot, that on being placed in dry grass, and blown upon, it takes fire;

with this, a large pile of wood is kindled, and allowed to burn a certain time. He then takes three nuts of an oily nature, called tootooee; having broken the shells, one of the kernels is thrown into the fire, at which time he says an anana, or prayer; and while the nut is crackling in the fire, repeats the words Muckeeroio kanaka ai kooee, that is, kill or shoot the fellow. The same ceremonies take place with each of the nuts, provided the thief does not appear before they are consumed.

This, however, but seldom happens; the culprit generally makes his appearence with the stolen property, which is restored to the owner, and the offence punished by a fine of four pigs. He is then dismissed, with strict injunctions not to commit the like crime in future, under pain of a more severe penalty. The pigs are taken to the morai, where they are offered up as sacrifices, and afterwards eaten by the priests.

Should it happen that the unfortunate criminal does not make his appearance during the awful ceremony, his fate is inevitable; had he the whole island to bestow, not one word of the prayer could be recalled, nor the anger of the Etooah appeased. The circumstance is reported to the king, and proclamation made throughout the island, that a certain person has been robbed, and that those who are guilty have been prayed to death.

So firm is their belief in the power of these prayers, that the culprit pines away, refusing to take any sustenance, and at last falls a sacrifice to his credulity.

The priests also practice medicine. Bathing is their great specific. If the patient is too weak to be carried to the sea, he is washed with salt water. The oil extracted from a nut, called tootooee, is used as a purgative; and a black mineral substance, reduced to a powder, as an emetic. This is very powerful in its effects; half the quantity that can be laid on a sixpence forming a sufficient dose.

I have but few particulars to give of their religious opinions. Their principal god, to whom they attribute the creation of the world, is called Etooah; and they have seven or eight subordinate deities, whose images are in the morai, and to whom offerings are made as well as to the Etooah. Their names I cannot recollect.

They believe in a future state, where they will be rewarded or punished for their conduct in this life. Their belief in the efficacy of prayer has already been remarked. During the time I lived with the king, it was reported that some person had prayed him to death; in order to counteract the effects of this, the daughter of a chief prostrated herself before the house, and turning towards the setting sun, prayed with great fervency. I did not then understand the language, and imagined that she was addressing that luminary; but William Moxely explained that part to me. She said, How could the sun rise and set, or the moon perform her revolutions, if there were not some superior Being who regulated their motions.

They have a tradition of a general deluge. According to their account, the sea once overflowed the whole world, except Mouna Kaa, in Owhyhee, and swept away all the inhabitants but one pair, who saved themselves on that mountain, and are the parents of the present race of mankind.

Their morais, or places of worship, consist of one large house, or temple, with some smaller ones round it, in which are the images of their inferior gods. The tabooed, or consecrated precincts, are marked out by four square posts, which stand thirty or forty yards from the building. In the inside of the principal house there is a screen or curtain of white cloth, hung across one end, within which the image of Etooah is placed. When sacrifices are offered, the priests and chiefs enter occasionally within this space, going in at one side and out at the other. Although present on one occasion, I did not enter this recess, partly because I was doubtful of the propriety of doing so, and also on account of the difficulty I had in moving myself, and the risk of getting my wounds injured among the crowd.

On the outside are placed several images made of wood, as ugly as can be well imagined, having their mouths all stuck round with dog's teeth.

Their holidays took place about four times a month, and the ceremonies lasted from sunset on the day preceding, to sunrise on the following day; during which no person was permitted to pass the bounds of the morai. This time was spent in prayer, in sacrificing pigs, in eating the sacrifices, and in conversation. I attended only once, and was not, at that time, sufficiently master of the language to understand the purport of the prayers.

The priest continued nearly three hours, in a very solemn manner, during which the most profound silence was observed; indeed, the smallest noise of any kind, either within the morai or in the neighbourhood, would have been a proof that the deity was offended, and the prayer must have ceased; a proclamation was, therefore, made by the public crier, whenever the king entered the morai, ordering every animal near it to be confined, otherwise they should be seized and offered up as sacrifices. Those present stood with their arms extended towards heaven for about three quarters of an hour at the beginning of the prayer, and the same length of time at its conclusion. I was not required to perform this part of the ceremony.

The number present did not exceed forty, and were all of the higher rank. Women are never permitted to attend on these occasions.

Human sacrifices are offered upon their going to war; but nothing of the kind took place during my stay; unless in the case already mentioned, of the man punished for breaking the taboo, and whose body was exposed before the idol.

During the period called Macaheite, which lasts a whole month, and takes place in November, the priests are employed in collecting the taxes, which are paid by the chiefs in proportion to the extent of their territories; they consist of mats, feathers, and the produce of the country. The people celebrate this festival by dancing, wrestling, and other amusements.

The king remains in the morai for the whole period; before entering it, a singular ceremony takes place. He is obliged to stand till three spears are darted at him: He must catch the first with his hand, and with it ward off the other two. This is not a mere formality. The spear is thrown with the utmost force, and should the king lose his life, there is no help for it.*

* Tamaahmaah is so dexterous in the use of the spear, that he probably runs little risk in thus exposing himself. Vancouver relates, that in a sham-fight he saw him ward off six spears that were hurled at him almost at the same instant. "Three he caught as they were flying with one hand; two he broke by parrying them with his spear; and the sixth, by a trifling inclination of his body, passed harmless"—*Vancouver*, Vol. III. p. 254.

At the Macaheite, which happened when I was on the island, the eldest son of Tamaahmaah, a youth about fifteen, was invested with royal honours, and entitled to the same marks of respect as his father. What share he had in the government I did not learn; but I observed no alteration in the exercise of the king's authority.

The houses of the natives are of the simplest form; they are oblong, with very low side-walls, and high-thatched roofs; within, they are not divided into separate apartments, nor have they any tables or seats.

It is only by size that the houses of the chiefs are distinguished from those of the lower orders, for the same barn-like shape is universal. They are, however, kept very clean; and their household utensils, consisting of wooden dishes and calabashes, are hung, neatly arranged, upon the walls. While the floors of the meaner houses are bare, except the place for sleeping, where a few mats are spread, those of the higher orders are entirely covered over with mats, many of which are worked with great elegance into different patterns. At one end, a platform raised about three feet from the ground, which extends the whole breadth of the apartment, is spread with a layer of rushes, and covered with mats. This forms the sleeping place for the upper part of the family; the attendants sleep at the opposite end.

As the two sexes never eat together, the chiefs have always a separte eating-house, and even the lower ranks have one to every six or seven families for the men. The women take their food in the same houses in which they sleep.

Few of the houses, except the largest, have any windows; the light being admitted by the door, which is seldom closed. The dwellings of the upper ranks are generally surrounded by a paling. In all of them the utmost attention to cleanliness prevails.

Their mode of cooking has been often described. Poey, or taro-pudding, which is the principal food of all ranks, is prepared by baking the root in a pit with hot stones, upon which water is poured. It is afterwards scraped, mashed, and mixed with cold water. When newly made, it is not unpalatable, but it soon turns sour.

Fish are often eaten raw, seasoned with salt water. When cooked, they are either done in their usual manner, under ground, or broiled, by putting them, wrapt in leaves, upon the fire. When the leaves are burnt, they consider them ready.

They preserve pork by taking out the bones, and rubbing it well with salt; after which it is made up in rolls, and dried.

They frequently eat with their pork a kind of pudding made of taro-root, which is previously cut in slices, and dried in the sun; it keeps a great length of time, and is a good substitute for bread. In this state it is preferred by the white people. The natives preserve it for taking to sea, by mashing and forming it into a solid paste, when it is wrapped in leaves, and will keep fresh for five or six weeks.

The sugar-cane, which they chew, is also a general article of food.

Instead of candles, the tootooee-nut is used, which being of an oily nature, yields a considerable quantity of light. It grows upon a small tree, and is about the size of a horse-chesnut. When pulled, they are thrown into water, and those that sink are reckoned sound; they are then baked under ground, and their shells broken off, in which state they are kept till required. When used as candles, they string twenty or thirty upon a slit of bamboo, each of which will burn five or six minutes ; but they require constant trimming, and it is necessary to reverse the torch whenever a nut is consumed, that the one under it may catch fire. It must, therefore, be held by a person whose business it is to keep it always in order.

This nut, when pressed, yields an oil well adapted for mixing with paint. The black colour, by which their canoes are painted, is produced by burning the nuts after they are pressed, and by the cinders of the torches, which are carefully preserved for the purpose ; these are reduced to powder, and mixed with oil.

Ava, with which the natives were formerly wont to intoxicate themselves, is now giving way to the use of ardent spirits. I never saw it used, except as a medicine to prevent corpulency, and is said to be an effectual remedy. It causes a white scurf to strike out upon the skin, somewhat like the dry scurvy.

The spirit distilled from the tea-root now usurps its place, and I fear the consequences will be still more pernicious.

That plant grows wild in the upper part of the country, and varies from the size of a carrot to that of a man's thigh. It is put into a pit, amongst heated stones, and covered with plantain and taro leaves; through these a small hole is made, and water poured in; after which the whole is closed up again, and allowed to remain twenty-four hours. When the root has undergone this process, the juice tastes as sweet as molasses. It is then taken out, bruised, and put into a canoe to ferment; and in five or six days is ready for distillation.

Their stills are formed out of iron pots, which they procure from American ships, and which they enlarge to any size, by fixing several tier of calabashes above them, with their bottoms sawed off, and the joints well luted. From the uppermost, a wooden tube connects with a copper cone, round the inside of which is a ring with a pipe to carry off the spirit. The cone is fixed into a hole in the bottom of a tub filled with water, which serves as a condenser.

By this simple apparatus a spirit is produced, called lumi, or rum, and which is by no means harsh or unpalatable. Both whites and natives are unfortunately too much addicted to it. Almost every one of the chiefs has his own still.

Smoking tobacco is another luxury of which the natives are very fond. The plant grows in abundance upon the islands, and they use it in a green state. In their tobacco pipes they display their usual taste and ingenuity. The tube is made of a hollow stem of a kind of vine, fixed to an iron bowl, which is inserted into hard wood. The stem is covered with rings of ivory and turtle-shell, placed alternately; the whole kept firmly together at the top by an ivory mouth-piece.

The women are subject to many restrictions from which the men are exempted. They are not allowed to attend the morai upon taboo days, nor at these times are they permitted to go out in a canoe. They are never permitted to eat with the men, except when at sea, and then not out of the same dish. Articles of delicacy, such as pork, turtle, shark, cocoa-nuts, bananas or plantains, are also forbidden. Dog's flesh and fish were the only kinds of animal food lawful for them to eat; but since the introduction of sheep and goats, which are not tabooed, the ladies have less reason to complain.

Notwithstanding the rigour with which these ceremonies are generally observed, the women very seldom scruple to break them, when it can be done in secret; they often swim off to ships at night during the taboo; and I have known them eat of the forbidden delicacies of pork and shark's flesh. What would be the consequence of a discovery I know not; but I once saw the queen transgressing in this respect, and was strictly enjoined to secrecy, as she said it was as much as her life was worth.

Their ideas of marriage are very loose; either party may quit the other when they tire or disagree. The lower classes in general, content themselves with one wife; but they are by no means confined to that number, and the chiefs have frequently several. Tamaahmaah had two, besides a very handsome girl, the daughter of a chief, educating for him. One elderly chief, Coweeooranee, had no fewer than fifteen. They are very jealous of any improper connexion between natives and their wives; but the case is widely different with respect to their visitors, where connexion of that kind is reckoned the surest proof of friendship, and they are always anxious to strengthen it by that tie.

The virtue of the king's wives is, however, most scrupulously guarded; each of them having a male and a female attendant, whose duty it is to watch them on all occasions. Should it be discovered that any of the queens have been unfaithful, these attendants are punished with death, unless they have given the first intimation.

Immediately after child-birth, women are obliged to retire to the woods, where they remain ten days, and must not be seen by the men. The queen, who had a daughter whilst I was there, had a house for the purpose of retirement; but, in general, they have no other shelter but what the woods afford. They also retire in the same manner three days in every month.*

* Captain Lisianski relates the same practice as prevalent among the Aleutian women: if he is not mistaken in ascribing it to them instead of the Sandwich islanders, or if our author has not fallen into the opposite error, the coincidence is remarkable.

Campbell, upon being questioned, related several instances of its having occurred in Wahoo. He cannot say as to the practice of the Aleutian islands.

A simple garment, called pow, forms the principal part of the dress of the women; it consists of a piece of cloth about one yard broad and three in length, wrapped several times round the waist, with the end tucked in below, and reaching to the calf of the leg. In cold weather, they throw another piece of cloth, like a plaid, over their shoulders. Round the neck they often wear wreaths of the leaves of a fragrant plant called miri, resembling those of the vine.

An ivory ornament, called palava, is very generally worn, suspended by a hair necklace, neatly plaited into small cords. The hole through which it is passed is large enough to admit the thumb, and the plaits are so numerous as to fill it entirely.

The hair is combed back in front, and plastered over with a kind of lime made from burnt shells. This practice bleaches that on the forehead nearly white.

Their heads are adorned with wreaths of flowers taken from the stalk, and strung on the stem of a small creeping plant. They prefer purple, yellow, and white, and arrange them alternately three or four inches of each colour. This is twined several times round the head, and has a very elegant appearance.

They are at great pains in ornamenting themselves, for which purpose every female is provided with a small mirror. All ranks pay the utmost attention to personal cleanliness.

The dress of the men consists merely of a small girdle, made of taper, called the maro. Upon great occasions, the chiefs wear elegant cloaks and helmets of red and yellow feathers.

The cloth called taper is entirely manufactured by women, and is made from a bark of a tree, which is first steeped in water, and then beat out with a piece of wood, grooved or furrowed like a crimping machine. The bark is laid upon another piece of wood, grooved like the former. As these two instruments are at right angles during the operation, the marks in the cloth are crossed like warp and woof.

It is colored with the juice of berries, laid on with a piece of turtle-shell, shaped like a knife, or with a brush, formed by chewing the end of a slip of bamboo. In this manner it is tinged brown, green, blue, and black; to produce a yellow, the cloth is dipt in a dye prepared by boiling the cone of a tree in water. They often paint a variety of patterns, in which they display great taste and fancy.

This cloth, from its texture, is, when wetted, extremely apt to get damaged, in which state it tears like moist paper; great care, therefore, is always taken to keep it dry, or to have it carefully dried when it is wetted. When they swim off to ships, they hold their clothes out of the water in one hand, occasionally changing it as it becomes fatigued.

The mats with which the floors of the houses are covered, are also manufactured by the women. They are made of rushes, or a kind of broad-leaved grass, split at the stem, and are worked in a variety of patterns.

The natives are most dexterous fishers, and their implements are constructed with much ingenuity. The hooks are sometimes made of mother-of-pearl and tortoise-shell, but those procured from ships are coming into more general use.

Their nets and lines are spun from the fibre of a broad-leaved plant called ourana, similar in appearance to sedge or flags; it is pulled green, and the outside stripped off with a tortoise-shell knife, after which it is steeped in water; the fibres are separated by the nail, and spun into lines, by rolling them between the hand and the thigh. The lines have sometimes two strands, and sometimes three, and are much stronger than those of hemp. They drag these lines after their canoes, and in this manner take bonettas, dolphins, and albicores. For the hooks of their own manufacture bait is not required, the mother-of-pearl shank serving the same end. When wire-hooks are used, they wrap a piece of white cloth round them.

The nets in which they take the flying fish are made of twine of the same material.—They are about a hundred yards in length, by three or four yards in breadth, and have a large bag in the centre.

They are set like herring-nets, with the upper edge floated by buoys of light wood, whilst the lower edge is kept under water by weights of lead or iron. In order to prevent the fish from flying over, branches of trees are laid all along the head-line. When properly extended, a canoe at each end of the net, gradually advances, forming it into a circle, into which the fish are driven by a number of canoes, who fill up the open side, and beat the surface violently with branches.—When the canoes at each end of the net meet, they gradually take it in, contracting the circle till the fish are forced into the bag in the centre.

In this manner prodigious numbers are taken. I have known them return, after a day's fishing, with ten or twelve canoes deeply loaded. Sometimes the net is so full they cannot take it on board, and are obliged to drag it after them to the shore.

They have a singular method of catching fish by poison. This is done by means of an herb like heath, stripped of its bark, and bruised; with this they dive to the bottom, and place it beneath the stones, where the fish lie. The poison is so powerful, that in a short time they sicken, and come up to the surface.—When taken they are instantly gutted, in order that the poison in their stomach may not affect the quality of the fish.

The occupiers or proprietors of land are entitled to the privilege of fishing upon their own shores as far as the tallest man in the island can wade at low water, and they may exercise that right at all seasons; but beyond that the sea is tabooed, except at two periods in the year, of six weeks each, during which unlimited fishing is allowed. At these times it is the general employment of the natives, and they cure enough to serve them through the tabooed season.

In every article of their manufacture these islanders display an extraordinary degree of neatness and ingenuity, considering the simplicity of the tools with which they work.

The tool in most general use is a kind of tomahawk, or adze, called toe; it was formerly made of hard polished stone, but is now universally made of iron. To form it, they lash a thin plate of iron, from one to four inches broad, and five or six long, to a branch which has a piece of the stem attached to it. Plane irons are much in request for this purpose; but the toe is frequently made of an old hoop.

This, with a piece of coral for a file, is almost the only tool used in the construction of their houses, canoes, and implements of wood.

The circular wooden dishes, containing from half a pint to five or six gallons, are formed with these simple tools, and are as neatly made as if they had been turned in a lathe. It is astonishing how soon they acquire the useful arts from their visitors. Many of the natives are employed as carpenters, coopers, blacksmiths, and tailors, and do their work as perfectly as Europeans.

In the king's forge there were none but native blacksmiths; they had been taught by the armourer of a ship, who quitted the island while I was there.

Almost all their dealings are conducted by barter; they know the value of dollars, and are willing to take them in exchange; but they seldom appear again in circulation, being always carefully hoarded up.

Vessels are supplied with fresh provisions, live-stock, salt, and other articles of outfit, for which they give in return cloth, fire-arms, and ammunition, the teeth of the sea-lion, carpenter's tools, hardware, and, in general, European articles of every description.

Sandal-wood, pearls, and mother-of-pearl shells, are also the produce of these islands, and are frequently purchased for the China market.

It is probable that the Russians will, in future, derive from hence the principal supplies of provisions for their settlements on the Fox islands, and northwest coast of America, and even Kamschatka.

With the island of Atooi the natives carry on a considerable trade. The inhabitants of Wahoo excel in making taper or cloth, whilst those of Atooi excel in canoes, paddles, and spears, and they very often make exchanges in these articles.

Owing to the number of ships that are constantly touching at these islands, provisions are by no means cheap. A pig is estimated by its length. The largest size, called poa-nana, or fathom pig, measures that length from the snout to the rump, and is valued at two axes; a junk of the thickest part of the sea-horse tooth, five or six inches long, a yard and a half of blue cloth, or five dollars.

Those that measure from the elbow to the opposite hand, are valued at one axe, or about half the price of the larger size. A sheep or goat may be had for a smaller piece of ivory; a maro, or a pair of fowls, for a knife, a pair of scissors, or small mirror.

From their earliest years, the natives spend much of their spare time in the water, and constant practice renders them so dexterous, that they seem as much at their ease in that element as on land; they often swim several miles off to ships, sometimes resting upon a plank shaped like an anchor stock, and paddling with their hands, but more frequently without any assistance whatever.

Although sharks are numerous in these seas, I never heard of any accident from them, which I attribute to the dexterity with which they avoid their attacks.

Throwing the top shoots of the sugar-cane at each other, and catching them in their flight, is a favorite amusement, the practice of which tends to render them very expert in the use of the spear.

Dancing, wrestling, and foot races, are also common amusements, particularly at macaheite time.

The dances are principally performed by women, who form themselves into solid squares, ten or twelve each way, and keep time to the sound of the drum, accompanied by a song, in which they all join. In dancing they seldom move their feet, but throw themselves into a variety of attitudes, sometimes all squatting, and at other times springing up at the same instant. A man in front with strings of shells on his ankles and wrists, with which he marks time, acts as fugel-man. On these occasions the women display all their finery, particularly in European clothes, if they are so fortunate as to possess any. They received great applause from the spectators, who frequently burst into immoderate fits of laughter, at particular parts of the song.

They have a game somewhat resembling draughts, but more complicated. It is played upon a board about twenty-two inches by fourteen, painted black, with white spots, on which the men are placed; these consist of black and white pebbles, eighteen upon each side, and the game is won by the capture of the adversary's pieces.

Tamaahmaah excels at this game. I have seen him sit for hours playing with his chiefs, giving an occasional smile, but without uttering a word. I could not play, but William Moxely, who understood it well, told me that he had seen none who could beat the king.

The game of draughts is now introduced, and the natives play it uncommonly well.

Flying kites is another favorite amusement. They make them of taper, of the usual shape, but uncommon size, many of them being fifteen or sixteen feet in length, and six or seven in breadth; they have often three or four hundred fathom of line, and are so difficult to hold, that they are obliged to tie them to trees.

The only employment I ever saw Tamena, the queen, engaged in, was making these kites.

A theatre was erected under the direction of James Beattie, the king's block-maker, who had been at one time on the stage in England. The scenes representing a castle and a forest were constructed of different coloured pieces of taper, cut out and pasted together.

I was present on one occasion, at the performance of Oscar and Malvina. This piece was originally a pantomime, but here it had words written for it by Beattie. The part of Malvina was performed by the wife of Isaac Davis. As her knowledge of the English language was very limited, extending only to the words yes and no, her speeches were confined to these monosyllables. She, however, acted her part with great applause. The Fingalian heroes were represented by natives clothed in the Highland garb, also made out of taper, and armed with muskets.

The audience did not seem to understand the play well, but were greatly delighted with the after-piece, representing a naval engagement. The ships were armed with bamboo cannon, and each of them fired a broadside, by means of a train of thread dipped in saltpetre, which communicated with each gun, after which one of the vessels blew up. Unfortunately, the explosion set fire to the forest, and had nearly consumed the theatre.

The ceremonies that took place upon the death of a chief have been already described. The bodies of the dead are always disposed of secretly, and I never could learn where they were interred. My patroness, the queen, preserved the bones of her father, wrapt up in a piece of cloth. When she slept in her own house they were placed by her side; in her absence they were placed on a feather bed she had received from the captain of a ship, and which was only used for this purpose. When I asked her the reason of this singular custom, she replied, "it was because she loved her father so dearly."

When the king goes to war, I understand that every man capable of bearing arms must follow his chief; for which purpose they are all trained from their youth to the use of arms. I saw nothing like a regular armed force, except a guard of about fifty men, who constantly did duty at the king's residence. There were about twenty of them on guard daily, but the only sentry which they posted was at the powder magazine. At night he regularly called out every hour, "All's well."

They were armed with muskets and bayonets, but had no uniform; their cartridge-boxes, which were made by the king's workmen, are of wood, about thirteen inches long, rounded to the shape of the body, and covered with hide.

I have seen those guards at their exercise; rapidity, and not precision, seemed to be their great object. The men stood at extended order, and fired as fast as they could, beating the butt upon the ground, and coming to the recover without using the ramrod; each man gave the word "fire," before he drew the trigger.

The natives of these islands have been accused of being cannibals; but as far as I could judge, either from my own observation, or from the enquiries I made, I believe the accusation to be perfectly destitute of foundation. Isaac Davis, who had the best means of knowing, having resided there more than twenty years, and who had been present and borne a share in all their wars, declared to me most pointedly, that " it was all lies—that there never had been cannibals there since they were islands."

From a perusal of the foregoing pages, it will be seen, that these islanders have acquired many of the useful arts, and are making rapid progress towards civilization. Much must be ascribed, no doubt, to their natural ingenuity and unwearied industry ; but great part of the merit must also be ascribed to the unceasing exertions of Tamaahmaah, whose enlarged mind has enabled him to appreciate the advantages resulting from an intercourse with Europeans, and he has prosecuted that object with the utmost eagerness.

The unfortunate death of captain Cook, and the frequent murders committed by the natives on navigators, particularly in Wahoo, in which Lieutenant Hengist, and Mr. Gooch, astronomer of the Dædalus, Messrs. Brown and Gordon, masters of the ships Jackall and Prince Le Boo, lost their lives, gave such ideas of the savage nature of the inhabitants, that for many years few ships would venture to touch at these islands.*

But since Tamaahmaah has established his power, he has regulated his conduct by such strict rules of justice, that strangers find themselves as safe in his port as in those of any civilized nation.

Although always anxious to induce white people to remain, he gives no encouragement to desertion, nor does he ever attempt to detain those who wish to depart.

In 1809 the king seemed about fifty years of age; he is a stout, well-made man, rather darker in the complexion than the natives usually are, and wants two of his front teeth. The expression of his countenance is agreeable, and he is mild and affable in his man-

* The editor has not thought himself at liberty to alter the orthography of the king's name adopted by Vancouver and Broughton. Although, to his ear, it would be more correctly Tameamea. Every voyager has spelt it in a different manner. Captain King has spelt it Maiha Maiha; Mr. Samwell, the surgeon of the Discovery, who published an account of Captain Cook's death, Cameamea; Portlocke, Comaamaa; Meares, Tomyhomyhaw; Vancouver and Broughton, Tamaahmaah; Lisianski, Hameamea; Langsdorf, Tomooma; and Turnbull, Tamahama. As the hard sound of *C* and *T* is scarcely to be distinguished in the pronunciation of the language, and the *h* is silent, the reader, from a comparison, will be able to ascertain the most correct way.

ners, and possesses great warmth of feeling; for I have seen him shed tears upon the departure of those to whom he was attached, and has the art of attaching others to himself. Although a conquerer, he is extremely popular among his subjects; and not without reason, for since he attained the supreme power, they have enjoyed repose and prosperity. He has amassed a considerable treasure in dollars, and possesses a large stock of European articles of every description, particularly arms and ammunition; these he has acquired by trading with the ships that call at the islands. He understands perfectly well how to make a bargain; but is unjustly accused of wishing to over-reach in his dealings. I never knew of his taking any undue advantages; on the contrary, he is distinguished for upright and honourable conduct in all his transactions.—War, not commerce, seems to be his principal motive in forming so extensive a navy. Being at peace, his fleet was laid up in ordinary during the whole time of my stay. When he chooses to fit it out, he will find no difficulty in manning his vessels. Independently of the number of white people he has constantly about him, and who are almost all sailors, he will find, even among his own subjects, many good seamen. He encourages them to make voyages in the ships that are constantly touching at the islands, and many of them have been as far as China, the northwest coast of America, and even the United States. In a very short time they become useful hands, and continue so as long as they remain in warm climates; but they are not capable of standing the effects of cold.

During my stay the building of the navy was suspended, the king's workmen being employed in erecting a house, in the European style, for his residence at Hanaroora. When I came away, the walls were as high as the top of the first story.

His family consisted of the two queens, who are sisters, and a young girl, the daughter of a chief, destined to the same rank. He had two sons alive, one about fifteen, and the other about ten years of age, and a daughter, born when I was upon the island.

The queen was delivered about midnight, and the event was instantly announced by a salute of sixteen guns, being a round of the battery in front of the house.

I was informed by Isaac Davis, that his eldest son had been put to death by his orders in consequence of criminal connexion with one of his wives. This took place before he fixed his residence at Wahoo.

His mode of life has already been described. He sometimes dressed himself in the European fashion, but more frequently laid aside his clothes, and gave them to an attendant, contenting himself with the maro. Another attendant carried a fan, made of feathers, for the purpose of brushing away the flies; whilst a third carried his spit-box, which was set round with human teeth, and had belonged, as I was told, to several of his predecessors.

It is said that he was at one time strongly addicted to the use of ardent spirits; but that, finding the evil consequences of the practice, he had resolution enough to abandon it. I never saw him pass the bounds of the strictest temperance.

His queen, Tamena, had not the same resolution; and although, when he was present, she durst not exceed, she generally availed herself of his absence in the morai to indulge her propensity for liquor, and seldom stopped short of intoxication. Two Aleutian women had been left on the island, and were favorite companions of hers. It was a common amusement to make them drunk; but, by the end of the entertainment, her majesty was generally in the same situation.

CHAPTER XI.

Departure from Wahoo—Pass Otaheite—Double Cape-Horn—Arrival at Rio Janeiro—Transactions there, during a residence of nearly two years—Voyage home—and from thence to the United States.

THE ship in which I left the Sandwich islands was called the Duke of Portland, commanded by captain Spence. She had procured a cargo of about one hundred and fifty tons of seal oil, and eleven thousand skins, at the island of Guadaloupe, on the coast of California, and had put into Wahoo for the purpose of procuring refreshments.

Every thing being ready, we sailed from Hanaroora on the 4th of March, and stood to the southward with pleasant weather.

In the beginning of April we descried the mountains of Otaheite, but did not touch at that island.

About a week before we doubled Cape Horn, we saw two large whales, and the boats were hoisted out in the hope of taking them, but it began to blow so hard that the attempt proved unsuccessful.

Early in May we passed Cape Horn; the captain stood as far south as the latitude of 60, and we never saw the land. Although the season was far advanced we did not experience the smallest difficulty in this part of the voyage.

A few days afterwards we made the Falkland islands; the land is of great height, and seems perfectly barren.

Upon the 25th we saw the coast of Brazil, and next day entered the harbour of Rio Janeiro.

Being apprehensive of a mortification in my legs, I applied for admission into the English hospital, which is situated in a small island that lies off the harbour. When captain Spence, who took me thither in his boat, mentioned that I had lost my feet in the service of the Americans, he was informed, that since that was the case, I must apply to them to take care of me.

I then went on board an American brig, called the Lion, the captain of which directed me to call on Mr. Baulch, the consul for that nation; by his interest I was admitted into the Portuguese hospital, *de la miserecordc.*

During the whole voyage I experienced the utmost attention and kindness from the captain and crew of the Duke of Portland; and when I quitted them they did not leave me unprovided for in a strange country; they raised a subscription, amounting to fifty dollars, which was paid into the hands of the Portuguese agent on my account.

I remained in the hospital ten weeks; the Portuguese surgeons, although they could not effect a cure, afforded me considerable relief, and I was dismissed as well as I ever expected to be.

I was now in a different situation from what I had been either at Kodiak or the Sandwich islands; I was in a civilized country, in which I must earn my subsistence by my own industry; but here, as well as there, I was under the protection of Divine Providence, and in all my misfortunes, I found friends who were disposed to assist me.

Mr. Baulch, the American consul, gave me a jar of the essence of spruce, which I brewed into beer; and having hired a negro with a canoe, I went about the ships, furnishing them with that, and other small articles of refreshment.

While engaged in this employment, I went on board the ship Otter, returning from the South Seas, under the command of Mr. Jobelin, whom I had seen in the same vessel at the Sandwich islands. He informed me that he had visited Wahoo a few months after my departure, and found all my friends in good health, except Isaac Davis, who had departed this life after a short illness.

In this manner I was not only enabled to support myself, but even to save a little money. I afterwards hired a house at the rent of four milreas a month, and set up a tavern and boarding house for sailors; this undertaking not proving successful, I gave it up for a butcher's stall, in which I was chiefly employed in supplying the ships with fresh meat. This business proved a very good one, and I was sanguine in my hopes of being able to raise a small sum; but an unfortunate circumstance took place, which damped all my hopes, and reduced me again to a state of poverty.

In the night of the 24th July, my home was broken into, and I was robbed of every farthing I had, as well as of all my clothes.

As the purchase of carcasses required some capital, I was under the necessity of giving up my stall for the present. I again took myself to my old trade of keeping a bum-boat, till I had saved as much as enabled me to set up the stall again.

I was much assisted by the good offices of a gentleman from Edinburgh, of the name of Lawrie, who resided in my neighbourhood; he took great interest in my welfare, and was of essential servicc by recommending me to ships, as well as by occasionally advancing a little money to enable me to purchase a carcase.

The state of my health, however, prevented me from availing myself of the advantages of my situation; the sores in my legs, although relieved, had never healed, and gradually became so painful as to affect my health, and render me unable to attend to any business.

In consequence of this, I determined to return home, in hopes of having the cure effectually performed in my native country.

On the 5th of February, 1812, I quitted Rio Janeiro, after a stay of twenty-two months. I came home in the brig Hazard, captain Anderson, and arrived in the Clyde on the 21st of April, after an absence of nearly six years.

After residing nearly four years in my native country, and having still a desire to visit the Sandwich islands, I left Scotland, in the American ship Independence, commanded by captain John Thomas, on the 3d of September, 1816, for New-York. We had sixty-three passengers, and after a very tedious voyage of fifty-three days, we arrived in good health at our port of destination. I had been led to believe that I should find no difficulty in getting a passage to the Sandwich islands from New-York; but after a short residence there, I did not see any prospect of obtaining a conveyance thither. My funds growing low, I commenced soliciting subscribers for my work. In this I met with considerable success, and was enabled to publish an edition of one thousand copies. But on account of the ulcers in my legs never healing, and being apprehensive of mortification, I was deterred from proceeding any farther. I therefore applied to the governors of the New-York city hospital for admittance, with the intention of having my legs amputated higher up, so that I might not be troubled with them in future. I was accordingly admitted on the 4th of November, 1817; and on the 20th of the same month, one of my legs was taken off a little below the knee. The second operation was performed on the 17th of January following; and I was enabled to leave the hospital on the 3d of April, 1818.

I still wished to return to the Sandwich islands, and having so far recovered as to be able to walk about with considerable ease, and the favourable appearance of my wounds indicating a thorough cure, I therefore made application to several gentlemen in New-York, by whose means my intentions were represented to the Prudential Committee of the American Board of Commissioners for Foregn Missions. By their advice I removed to the institution belonging to that body, at Cornwall, Litchfield county, Connecticut, in order that I might there study under the Rev. Herman Daggett, and that I might become acquainted with several young men, in that place from the Sandwich islands; to the end, that if ever it should please Divine Providence to permit me to visit those islands again, I might be able to render them and the cause of religion, all the assistance that lay in my power, and that my influence might be exerted on the side of virtue; and, above all things, that I might be instrumental in forwarding the introduction of missionaries into those dark and benighted islands of the sea.

APPENDIX.

VOCABULARY

OF THE

LANGUAGE OF THE SANDWICH ISLANDS.

APPENDIX No. I.

A VOCABULARY

OF THE

LANGUAGE OF THE SANDWICH ISLANDS.

In pronouncing the words as spelt in the vocabulary, *all letters must be sounded,* with the exceptions after mentioned.

In sounding the vowels, A has always the sound of the initial and final letter in the word *Arabia.*

E, as in the word *eloquence,* or the final Y in *plenty.*

The double E, as in *keep.*

I, as in the word *indolence.*

O, as in the word *form.*

The double O, as in *boot, good.*

U, as in the word *but.*

The diphthongs Ai, as the vowel sounds in *tye, fly,* or the I in *diameter.*

Ei, as in the word *height.*

Oi, as in the word *oil.*

Ow, as in the word *cow.*

All other combinations of vowels are to be sounded separately; thus, *oe, you,* and *roa, distant,* are dissyllables.

In sounding the consonants, H is always aspirated; the letters K and T, L and R, B and P, are frequently substituted for each other.

Thus, *kanaka, tanata,* people; *ooroo, ooloo,* bread-fruit; *bou, poa,* a hog.

Where the words are separated by a comma, they are synonymous, and either may be used; but where there is no comma, both must be used.

Example. *Taate, Keike tanne,* a boy.

It frequently happens that the same word is repeated twice, in which case it is connected with a hyphen; thus *leepe-leepe,* an axe.

A

Above	*Aroona*
Adze	*Toe*
Afraid	*Macaoo*
After me, come	*Mamooraao, peemaio*
Afterwards	*Mamoore*
Agreable	*Nawee-nawee*
American, an	*Tanata, Merikana*
Angry	*Hoohoo*
Arm, the	*Poheva*
Arrow	*Eeoome*
Ashore	*Ayooka*
At	*Eia*
Avaricious	*Peepere*
Aunt	*Titooa waheine*
Axe	*Leepe-leepe*
Apple	*O.ieea*

B

Back, the	*Tooata*
Back, to carry on	*Eoaha*
Bad	*Eeno, heva, nooe-nooe heva*
Bad man	*Kanaka poopoota*
Bald	*Oopoboota*
Bamboo	*Ohe*
Bark	*Hohore*
Battle	*Emutta*
Bed	*Moena*
Beard	*Oome-oome*
Beat a drum, to	*Erokoo*
Bee	*Narro*
Bees wax	*Tootai narro*
Begone	*Hiere piero oe*
Behind	*Temoore*
Belly	*Manaoo, opoo*
Belch	*Erooee*
Below	*Deerro*
Between	*Feropoo*
Bird	*Mannoo*
Biscuit	*Bikete*
Bitter	*Ava-ava*
Black	*Ere-ere*
Bladder	*Toa-meeme*
Blind	*Muka pa*
Block, pully	*Pockaka*
Blood	*Toto*
Board, or plank to swim on	*Papa*
Board, on	*Aroona*
Bone	*Oohe*

Bonetta, a fish so called	*Pehe rera*
Bottom	*Okoree*
Bowl, wooden	*Apoina*
Boy	*Taate, keike tannee*
Boy, a familiar way of speaking	*Heimanne*
Bracelet of shells	*Teepoo*
Bread fruit	*Ooroo-ooloo*
Break, to	*Anaha*
Breast	*Ooma*
Blue	*Ooree-ooree*
Bring me	*Peemai*
Broken	*Motoo*
Brother	*Keike tanee*
Brown	*Aoora oora*
Bucket	*Tabahoo*
Button	*Opeehee, booboo*
Buttons, string of	*Porcema*
Buy, to	*Tooai*

C

Cabbage	*Tabete*
Calabash	*Areepo*
Calm	*Maneeno*
Cannon	*Poo nooee*
Canoe, single	*Evaha*
Canoe, double	*Makarooa*
Captain of a ship	*Eree te motoo*
Care, to take	*Malamma*
Carry, to	*Famo*
Cat	*Bobokee*
Cheerful	*Warra-warra*

Cheeks	*Papareena*
Chief	*Eree*
Chest	*Pahe*
Chicken	*Moa tina*
Child	*Keike, kumaree*
Child-bearing	*Hemo te keike*
Cider	*Wyoheea*
Clean	*Ooama*
Cloak, or upper garment	*Teaboota, tapa*
Cloth, also clothes	*Tapa*
Cloth-plant	*Eaootee*
Circumcision	*Poohe*
Cock	*Moa tannee*
Cockroach	*Patte-patte*
Cocoa nut	*Caneeo*
Cold	*Anoo*
Come	*Here*
Come here	*Here mai*
Come with me	*Peemai taroo*
Contempt, a term of	*Poopoota, poopooka*
Conversation	*Para paroo*
Cooked, or baked	*Oomoaroa*
Coyness in a woman	*Nonoa*
Cough, to	*Ehapoo*
Country the	*Ayooca*
Country, foreign, generally applied to Britain	*Caheite*
Cow	*Peepe-nooe*
Crab	*Pappee*
Crab, particular kinds of	*Epootoo, pehoo*
Cray fish	*Pehe oora*
Crimsou	*Oora-oora*

Cry to, or weep	*Taee*
Cured, it is	*Oraroa*
Cut, to	*Hakee-hakee*

D

Dance, to	*Ehoora-hoora*
Dark	*Poa rere*
Day	*Poa*
Day, to	*Aeea poa*
Dead	*Makeroa*
Delicious	*Honnoo onnoo*
Demon, or devil	*Etooa heva*
Dig, to	*Maiai*
Dirt	*Totai, erepo*
Distant	*Roa, maroa*
Dive, to	*Eehopoo-poo*
Dog	*Edea cao*
Dolphin	*Oona*
Door	*Poola*
Done, or finished	*Poaroa*
Drink, to	*Aeeno*
Drunk	*Honnoo*
Drum	*Pahoo*
Duck	*Mora*
Dusk, or twilight	*Hoi-hoi te poa*
Dwell, to	*Enoho*

E

Earth	*Ehonooa*
Ears	*Pepeaoo, tareea*

Eat, to	*Eeai*
Eels, or sea-snakes	*Hoohe*
Egg	*Ehooeero*
Egg, sea	*Neeootai*
England	*Pritane, Kaheite*
Englishman	*Kanaka Pritane, Kanaka Kaheite*
Enough	*Maoona*
Enter, to	*Marokonai*
Evening	*Ahee-ahee*
European	*Ehoorei*
Eyes	*Maka*
Eyebrow	*Tooa maka*
Excrement	*Tootai*

F

False	*Waha he, heva*
Fan, a	*Taheina*
Fan, to	*Taharee*
Father	*Mokooa tanne*
Fathom	*Anana*
Farewell	*Aroho-oe*
Pat	*Peea*
Fear	*Matao*
Feathers	*Hooroo, hooroo manno*
Feather necklace	*Araia*
Feeble	*Faeera*
Feet	*Wawye*
Female	*Waheine*
Fetch hither	*Heire mai, peemai*
Fin of a fish	*Tirra pehe*

Fine	*Eahe*
Fingers	*Tereema*
Fish	*Pehe*
Fish, a particular kind of	*Ava*
Flying fish	*Pehe orera*
Fish, to	*Ehootee*
Fist	*Amootoo*
Flat	*Papa*
Flea	*Ookoo rere*
Flower, a	*Pooa mono*
Fly, to	*Arere*
Fly, a	*Enarra*
Forgot	*Ooaro*
Fowl	*Moa*
Fresh	*Onoo*
Friend	*Heitanne, poonarooa*
Fruit	*Hooero*

G

Garment worn by the women	*Paoo*
Generous	*Horoa*
Girdle	*Tatooa*
Girdle worn by the men	*Maro*
Girl	*Keike waheina*
Give, to	*Mukunna*
Go	*Heire*
Goat	*Peepe Koa*
God	*Etooa*
Good	*Meitei*
Good morning	*Myty kakee aka*
Good night	*Myty ahee ahee*

Grandfather	*Poopooa tanne*
Grandmother	*Topooa waheine*
Gray	*Aheena heena*
Grass	*Moo*
Grass, broad leaved, of which lines and nets are made	*Oorana*
Grasshopper	*Pepe rera*
Great	*Nooe-nooe*
Green	*Omomoo*
Gun	*Poo*

H

Hair	*Lavo hoo*
Handkerchief	*Haneeka*
Hands	*Reema*
Handsome	*Meitei*
Harbour	*Aeeva, too-too*
Hard	*How*
Haste, make	*Weete-weete*
Has, past time	*Roa*
Hat	*Paparee*
Have	*Havee*
Head	*Po*
He or she	*Oera*
Hearing	*Faro*
Heart	*Ehottoo, teate*
Heat, or hot	*Mahanna*
Heat of the sun	*Mahanna ke Laoo*
Helmet	*Mayoree*
Hen	*Moa waheine*

Herb, used by white people for tea	*Nehe*
Here	*Mai*
Hermaphrodite	*Mahoo*
Hide, to	*Ehoona*
High	*Roehee*
Hill	*Parei*
Hog	*Poa, boa*
Hold your tongue	*Koore-koore oe*
Hole	*Pooka*
Hook for fishing	*Mattoo*
Hook, made of ivory, worn as an ornament	*Palava*
Horse	*Edea nooee*
House	*Harree, eharee*
House (sleeping)	*Harre, moe*
House (eating)	*Harre eai*
How are you	*Arohooe*
Hungry	*Porore*
Husband	*Tanne*

I

I, my, or me	*Waoo, tawa*
Jacket	*Teakete*
Interjection of grief	*Aroha eenoo*
Interjection of admiration	*Taa ha ha*
Iron	*How*
Island	*Motoo*
Itch, to	*Mairo*

K

Keep	*Vaihee*
Kill	*Papahee, matte-matte make-roa*
King	*Eree nooee*
Knife	*Okee-okee, kanee-kanee*
Know	*Nono, eete*

L

Lame	*O-opa*
Land	*Ayooka*
Land cultivated	*Aiena*
Laugh	*Aitaha*
Lazy	*Moolawa*
Lean, not fat	*Amapoo*
Legs	*Wawye*
Let me see	*Meene-meene, nanna*
Lie, to tell a	*Poone-poone*
Light, not heavy	*Eamma*
Lightning	*Heaweetoh*
Lines	*Towra*
Lips	*Lehe-lehe*
Little	*Pekene, oo ookoo*
Lizard	*Moo*
Look	*Meere-meere*
Looking-glass	*Anee-anee*
Loss	*Moomooka*
Lost	*Ooreiro*
Louse	*Ookoo*

M

Male	*Tanee*
Man	*Tanata, tanee*
Man that eats with women	*Tanata inoa*
Many	*Maoena*
Maried, to be	*Noho te Waheina*
Marshmallow	*Etooa rere*
Mat	*Ahoo, moena*
Melon	*Ipoopeena*
Mine, my own	*Maooa, mao*
Month	*Malama*
Moon	*Maheina*
Moon, new	*Maheina erimai*
Moon, full	*Maheina nooee*
Morrow, to	*Apopo*
Morning	*Aheea pa*
Mother	*Makooa waheine*
Mountain	*Parei, parei nooee*
Mouth	*Waha*
Music	*Heeva*
Musket	*Poo*
Mustard	*Totai Kumaree*

N

Nail	*How*
Naked	*Tutarra*
Name	*Einoa*
Native of the islands	*Kanaka mowree*
Nasty	*Ereporepo*
Navel	*Petto*
Net	*Oopaka*

Night, this	*Aheeapo, arere*
No, not	*Aoaree*
Noon	*Akeia*
Nose	*Eehoo*
Nut, used to give light	*Tootooee*

O

Oar, or paddle	*Hoe*
Ocean	*Tai*
Of	*Te*
Old	*Emotoo, baheeoo*
Otaheitan	*Kanaka boolla-boolla*
Oven, or pit for cooking	*Eomoo*

P

Painting, printing, drawing, or writing	*Purra-purra*
Palm of the hand	*Apooreema*
Parent	*Makooa*
Pearl	*Mummee*
Pearl-river	*Wai mummee*
People	*Kanaka, tanata*
Perhaps (affirmatively)	*Ai pa*
——— (negatively)	*Ooree pa*
Pig	*Poa*
Pigeon	*Eroope*
Pinch, to	*Ooma*
Place of worship	*Morai*
Plank	*Papa*
Plantain	*Maio*
Plantation	*Aina*

Play, to	*Ehanne*
Pleasant	*Nawee-nawee*
Plenty	*Aroo-aroo, Maoona*
Pluck, to	*Hootee-hootee*
Potatoes, sweet	*Oowarra*
Prayer	*Poore, anana*
Priest	*Kahoona*
Present, or gift	*Makunna*
Presently	*Areea, mamoore*
Pressing with the hand when tired	*Rorome*
Prohibition	*Taboo*
Puncturation	*Tattoo*
Putrid	*Peea-peea*

Q

Quickly	*Weete-weete*

R

Rain	*Eooa*
Rat	*Eoree*
Red	*Oora-oora*
Remember, to	*No-no*
Ringworm, a disease	*Enooa*
Ripe	*Purra*
Ropes	*Toura*
Rotten	*Purra roa*
Row, to	*Ehoe*
Rum	*Lumma*
Rushes	*Anonoho*
Russian	*Tonata Lokeene*

S

Sailor	*Kanaka hanna-hanna te motoo*
Salt	*Pakai*
Salute, by joining noses	*Hone-hone*
Satisfied	*Maoona*
Saw, a	*Pahe oroo*
Scissors	*Oopa*
Sea	*Tai, wai tai*
Sea-snake	*Poohe*
Sea-egg	*Neeootai*
See, to	*Meene-meene*
Shark	*Manno*
Sheep	*Peepe*
Show me	*Meere-meere*
Ship	*Motoo*
Shine	*Peenoo-peenoo*
Shoot, to	*Mackeroa*
Shore	*Ayookee*
Shortly	*Mamooree*
Shut	*Oopa*
Sickness, or sore	*Mai, Poonine*
Sit, to, or squat	*Noho*
Sky	*Heiranei*
Sleep	*Moe-moe*
Small	*Ete*
Soldier	*Kanaka etooa*
Song	*Heeva*
Spade, wooden	*Maiai*
Speak, to	*Nummee-nummee*
Speech, or harangue	*Oraro*

Spear	*Pahoo, pahe*
Spit, to	*Too harre*
Spread, to	*Hohora*
Star	*Ehetoo*
Stay, wait a little	*Areea*
Steal, to	*Ei hooee*
Stink	*Peero-peero*
Stockings	*Tokeine*
Stone	*Pohakoo keeva*
Stool, to lay the head on when asleep	*Papa rooa*
Storm	*Teeooe-teoo*
Stranger	*Tanata howree*
Stop	*Marrea*
Sugar-cane	*To, ko*
Sun	*Laoo*
Surf of the sea	*Horoo tai*
Surgeon	*Nai*
Sweet	*Lea-lea, onno*
Swim	*Eaoo*

T

Tallow	*Oila*
Take, to	*Laiva, ooleva*
Take off, to	*Hemo*
Take care	*Malamma*
Tall	*Hoa*
Taro pudding	*Poe*
Teeth	*Neehoo*
Tell	*Ectee, nummee-nummee*
That	*Mao*

The	*Te, he, ke*
Thief	*Tanata ihooee*
Think, to	*No-no*
This	*Aeia, Aheea*
Tongue	*Alaloo*
Twins	*Teetee*
Twisting, in dancing,	*Amee-amee*

V

Very	*Nooee-nooee*

U

Uncle	*Titooa tannee*
Understand	*Eetee*
Understanding	*Nono*
Undress, to	*Hemo tapa*

W

Warm	*Mahanna*
Water	*Wai*
Water (fresh)	*Wai onnoo*
Water (salt)	*Wai tai*
Water, to make	*Meeme*
Weak	*Faeera*
We	*Taooa*
Wet	*Purra*
What	*Ehara*
What is your name	*Owhyt oe einoa*
Where	*Awaya*

Where have you been	*Yahea oee*
White	*Keeo-keeoo*
White people	*Tanata howree*
Why	*Tehala*
Wind	*Matanee*
Wish	*Mukee-mukee*
Within	*Maro koo*
With me	*Ta wa*
Woman	*Waheine*
Woman (married)	*Waheine mow*
Wont, I	*Aoohee*
Wood	*Tooheihe*
Work, to	*Hanna-hanna*
Wounded	*Tooitahe*
Wrong, you are	*Waha hai*

Y

Yam	*Oohee*
Yawn	*Poowha*
Year	*Makaheite*
Yellow	*O peeta-peeta*
Yes	*Ai*
You	*Oe*
Your	*Kow*

NUMERALS.

One	*Atahee*
Two	*Arooa*
Three	*Akoroo*
Four	*Ahea*

Five	*Areema*
Six	*Ahonoo*
Seven	*Aheitoo*
Eight	*Awarroo*
Nine	*Ivee*
Ten	*Oome*
Eleven	*Oome toome atahee*
Twelve	*Oome toome arooa*
Thirteen	*Ome toome akoroo*
Fourteen	*Oome toome ahaa*
Fifteen	*Oome toome areema*
Sixteen	*Oome toome ahonoo*
Seventeen	*Oome toome aheitoo*
Eighteen	*Oome toome awarroo*
Nineteen	*Oome toome ivee*
Twenty	*Kanna roa*
Thirty	*Kanna koroo*
Forty	*Atahee kannaha*
Eighty	*Arooa kannaha*
	&c. &c.
1600 or 40 × 40	*Ataha manno*
3200	*Arooa manno, &c.*

DIALOGUES.

Where are you going	*Awaya heire oe*
I am going on board the ship	*Heire waoo aroona te metoo*
I am going ashore	*Heire waoo ayooka*
I wish you to go	*Mukee-mukee heire waoo*
Very well, can you go with me	*Meitei, heire oe tawa*

No, the captain will not let me go	*Oaree pa, eree te motoo oaree mukee-mukee waoo heire*
There will be no work on board to-morrow	*Apopo taboo, oaree hanna-hanna aroona te motoo*
Very well, will you go to-morrow	*Meitei, heire oe apopo*
I cannot tell	*Oaree pa eetee waoo*
Where is the king	*Awaya te eree nooee*
He is gone on board the ship	*Heire roa aroona te motoo*
Has he taken any hogs on board	*Oolava poa aroona te motoo*
No; but he will take plenty when he goes ashore	*Oaree, mamooree peemai ayooka lavee nooee-nooee te poa*
The captain wishes to purchase a great many hogs	*Eree te motoo mukee-mukee tooai nooee te poa*
The ship sails to-morrow	*Apopo heire te motoo*
Where is she bound to	*Heire awaya*
She is bound for England	*Heire Kaheite*, or *Heire Pritane*
Will you go ashore, and sleep at my house	*Heire oe ayooka moe-moe to hare waoo*
I will see in a little	*Mamooree meene-meene waoo*
Come hither. Go on shore, and tell the king that the captain wishes to purchase a great many pearls	*Peemai oe, heire ayooka numme-numme te eree nooee, eree te motoo mukee tooai maoona te mummee*
I will go soon	*Mamooree heire waoo*
Mind that you remember	*Malamma kow no-no*
Do you know where the king is	*Eetee oe awaya te eree nooee*
He is gone to the Morai	*Ooheire marokoo te Morai*

William Stevenson, literally Lean William	*Willama Amapoo*
John Young	*Alhanna*
Isaac Davis	*Itseeke*
John Hairbottle literally Lame John	*Keone o-opa*
William Wordsworth, literally Hardbottom	*Willama Okoree how*
James Stow, literally James Large Brow	*Keeme Laoo Nooee*
James Beatty, literally the Block maker	*Keeme Hanna Pockaka*
The Author's name, literally Loss of the Feet	*Moomooka te Wawyee*

APPENDIX No. II.

STATEMENT

OF THE

CASE OF ARCHIBALD CAMPBELL.

BY DR. NORDGOORST,

IN THE SERVICE OF THE RUSSIAN AMERICAN COMPANY.

[Translated from the Russian.]

STATEMENT

OF THE

CASE OF ARCHIBALD CAMPBELL.

THE bearer hereof, named Archibald Macbrait, has had the misfortune to have both of his feet frostbitten in so dreadful a manner, that nothing remained but to endeavour to save his life, as there were no hopes whatever of preserving his feet, although every attempt was made to that effect.

For the information of the humane and benevolent, I subjoin a short statement of my proceedings in his case, fearless of any compunctions of conscience; being sensible of the hard fate of this poor fellow creature, and how much he stands in need of assistance to support his existence.

This Englishman sailed from Kodiak in the winter time, in the ship's cutter, for the island of Sannack. On their passage a storm came on, in which the boat was wrecked. The crew saved their lives on shore; but this man had both his feet frozen, and not having stripped off his clothes for twenty-seven days, he was not aware of the extent of his calamity, and did not apprehend the destruction of his feet.

The overseer of the district of Karlutzki brought him to Kodiak, at eight o'clock in the evening, to the hospital called the Chief District College of Counsellor and Chevalier Baranoff.

In the first place, I had his feet cleaned and dried; they were both in a state of mortification *(gangrena sicca.)* The mortified parts having separated from the sound to the distance of a finger's breadth, where either amputation might take place or a cure be performed, as the patient himself hoped. I dressed the mortified, or frostbitten parts with oil of turpentine, and the unaffected parts with olive oil, and continued these applications for about five days, after which I used charcoal, gas, and other chimical applications; but as there appeared no chance of saving his feet, I began to consider that there was no resourse left but amputation. That the patient might not be alarmed, I talked over the matter with him as is usual in such cases, and endeavoured to persuade him to submit to the operation, as the only means of effecting a cure. But at first I was not successful, and could not get him to agree to it. I was therefore obliged to continue my former mode of treatment. At the end of three days, however, he gave his consent, and I fixed a time for the operations, which I performed satisfactorily. On the third day after the operation, the wound appeared to be in a good state, and I continued to dress it daily as it required.

The other foot remained to undergo a similar operation. I suffered three weeks to elapse, when it also took place. The wounds are now in a good state, and evidently healing up.

It is not in my power to complete the cure, being obliged to return to Russia; but I have left the directions with the assistant surgeon how to proceed in the treatment.

The illness of Archibald Macbrait, this Englishman, commenced on the 22d of January, 1808. The first opera tion took place on the 15th of March, and the second on the 15th of April. He is twenty years of age, and well made. He was cured by Dr. Nordgoorst, actually in the service of the Russian American Company.

This statement should support the petition of this Englishman, who may seek an asylum in Greenwich hospital, where the unfortunate of this kind obtain relief and comfort.

N. B. This is an accurate description of the case and treatment; but the true christian name and surname of the patient, is Archibald Campbell.*

* The postscript was added in Latin, at the request of the author, when the surgeon read the case to him, Archibald Macbride being the name he assumed when he entered the American ship. *Vide* p. 17.

APPENDIX No. III.

NOTICE OF

ARCHIBALD CAMPBELL,

AUTHOR OF THE VOYAGE ROUND THE WORLD.

NOTICE OF

ARCHIBALD CAMPBELL.

[From Blackwood's Magazine.]

OUR readers cannot have forgotten the name of Archibald Campbell, the poor Scottish seaman, whose account of his voyage round the world was, three or four years ago, noticed at considerable length in the Quarterly Review. This unhappy adventurer's narrative was, in every way, well deserving of the interest which it created at the time of its publication. It was modest and unassuming in its manner, and, in its matter, free to a great extent, from the many species of blunders and inaccuracies which are commonly so abundant in the productions of persons in the humble situation of life of Archibald Campbell. At that time, however, its merits could not be quite so fully appreciated as now. Although the apparent candour of the mariner was well qualified to lend credit to all his statements, yet even his benevolent editor abstained from expressing himself in any very decided manner respecting their authority, and the same diffidence was, of course, shared by his reviewer. But in the years which have now intervened, the narratives of succeeding voyages have given perfect confirmation to all the assertions of Campbell; and his story may, therefore, be considered as forming an authentic link in the history of the Sandwich Islands, with regard to which, for several years previous to his arrival there, we had received no certain or direct intelligence.

We refer to Campbell's book itself, and the review of it already mentioned, for any information which our readers may require in order to restore them to a perfect acquaintance with the early and important incidents in his various life. At the time when his book was published, it will be recollected, the sores upon his legs were still in a very distressing condition, owing to the unskilful manner in which they had been amputated below the ankle, by the Russian Surgeon, into whose hands he fell immediately after they were frostbitten. The period of tranquil existence which he had spent in the Sandwich islands, the voyage homewards, and a residence of many months in his native country, had all been found insufficient to remove the irritation of his wounds; and he was still not only a cripple, but an acute sufferer, when he attracted the attention of Mr. Smith, in the Clyde steam-boat. The kindness of that excellent person soon enabled him to lay the story of his afflictions before the public, and the success of the book was such, as to furnish a sum far beyond the expectations of Archibald Campbell. Had he remained in this country during the time when the public impression was strongly in his favour, there is reason to believe that something might probably have been done to provide the means of comfortable retirement to one whose errors, in themselves venial, had been so severely punished in the person of the offender, and had furnished a lesson so capable of doing good to others. Neither Campbell nor his friends, however, entertained, at the moment, any expectations of such a nature, and the poor man, whose patience was quite exhausted, resolved, as soon as he got a little money into his hands, to seek in it the means of being once more transported to the friendly territories of king Tamaahmaah, and his own comfortable farm on the banks of the Wymumme. In the midst of all his distresses, he found leisure for courtship, so he set sail with his wife, in the autumn of 1816, for New-York, in the hope of finding a passage to Owhyhee, on board of some of the American ships, which have, of late years, been almost the only visitors of these islands. On the 23d of December following, he writes as follows, to a medical gentleman in Glasgow, who had shown him much kindness while in that city :—"I am very sorry to inform you that we shall have no opportunity of going to the Sandwich Islands this season, the vessels having all left Boston for the northwest coast before our arrival, and it is very likely that there will be no more ships going that way until they return again, which will not be these two years; therefore I am at a loss what to do. There is nothing at all doing here in my line, and times are much worse here than at home, and a great many of the passengers that came out with us have gone home again, not being able to find work of any kind." He then states his intention to procure, if possible, a passage to the Brazils, where he had before been. In the meantime, however, it was announced that some person was about to publish an American edition of his book, which unhandsome procedure Archibald forthwith took the most effectual method of preventing, by publishing an American edition of it himself. Of this edition he sold 700 copies in a month, and cleared about 300 dollars on the speculation.

His legs continued all this time to be as troublesome as ever; and Campbell determined to give himself a chance of being a sound cripple, by having them amputated over again above the ankle. This resolution he carried into effect last winter with the most perfect fortitude. His right leg was amputated on the 20th of November, 1817, and the bursting of an artery a few hours after the operation, threw him into a brain fever, from which he escaped with difficulty. "My whole leg," says he, "began from the end of the stump to be inflamed with erysipalas, combined with phlegmatic inflammation, which, luckily for me, turned into a suppuration. I am happy to inform you, that ever since, I have been mending so fast, that I was able to go home all last week, and it is only yesterday, (January 13, 1818) that I returned to have the other leg cut; and the surgeon says I shall have a better chance of recovery, as my habit is not so full." The second operation was accordingly performed in a few days after this, and his recovery was even more easy than he had been led to expect. "As soon as I got out of the hospital," says he, "I made myself a pair of artificial legs, with which I already begin to walk pretty tolerably, and am going to Albany, Baltimore, &c. to get subscriptions for the second edition of my book."

But during his stay in New-York, Campbell has not been an author, publisher, and patient only. He has also been carrying on various little species of traffic, in globe glass mirrors, plaster of Paris casts, Scots Almanacks, &c. &c. with various, but, on the whole, not very flattering success. As soon as he shall have sufficiently supplied the transatlantic reading public with his voyage round the world, Archy, who is a Jack of many trades, purposes to turn another of his talents to a little advantage, and to make a voyage to the Clyde "to see his friends," in the capacity of a cook to a merchantman. He still, however, has a hankering after his "steading" in Owhyhee; and it is probable that ere long we shall have it in our power to inform our readers that he has come to "his ain again."

We might quote some farther passages from his letters to his friend in Glasgow; but although they are all highly interesting to those who have seen any thing of the man, we are apprehensive of trespassing too far on the patience of the general reader. The letters are written in a clear, distinct style, and in a very good penmanship; and his account of the state of things in America, so far as it goes, shows that Archibald has been in his youth no inattentive or unworthy member of some of the "literary and commercial" clubs, so common in the west of Scotland. The letters are all concluded in a very polite manner, as thus:—"Be pleased, Sir, to give our best respects to your father and sisters, and our compliments to your servant maids; meantime, we remain, Sir, your most obedient and very humble servants,

ARCHB. & ISABELLA CAMPBELL."

We trust our readers will pardon us for detaining them so long with the history of this poor countryman of ours.— Those of them who have read his book will, we are quite sure, be happy in this renewal of their acquaintance with him; for our own parts, we hope he will, on his arrival, forthwith publish a full account of his adventures during this last voyage. He must now be pretty well initiated into the ways of the booksellers, and we do not see why Mr. Campbell should not succeed as well in his transactions with that slippery generation, as many other authors of greater pretension

APPENDIX, No. IV.

HISTORICAL ACCOUNT

OF THE

SANDWICH ISLANDS.

HISTORICAL ACCOUNT

OF THE

SANDWICH ISLANDS.

When captain Cook discovered the Sandwich islands, in 1778, Tereoboo was king of Owhyhee ; Titeree, of Moratai; and Pereoranne, of Wahoo, and the islands to leeward. The sovereignty of Mowee was contested by Tereoboo and Titeree ; the former claimed it for his son, who had married the daughter of the deceased king; the latter claimed it as heir male to the former sovereign. In consequence of this dispute, these chiefs were engaged in war at the above mentioned period; but captain King understood, before he quitted the islands, that an arrangement had taken place, by which Titeree retained Ranai Taharoora, whilst Mowee was ceded to Tewarro, the son of Tereoboo. Tamaahmaah, the present king, is known in Cook's Voyage by the name of Maiha-Maiha, and was present at the death of that illustrious navigator. He was the eldest son of Kaihooa, only brother to Tereoboo, and after his son, Tewarro, next heir to the succession.

After the departure of the Resolution and Discovery, no ships touched at the Sandwich islands till the year 1787. During the interval that had elapsed, considerable revolutions had taken place. Tereoboo was dead, and his dominions shared between his sons, Tewarro and Tamaahmaah; and Titeree had conquered the islands of Mowee and Wahoo.

The accounts of these transactions, owing to the few opportunities of inquiry which the navigators who touched at these islands enjoyed, and their ignorance of the language, are extremely contradictory.

By one account, Tereoboo is said to have been put to death by Tamaahmaah; by another, that he fell in battle; and by a third, that he died a natural death. The causes of the division of his territory between his son and nephew are involved in equal obscurity.

The ship Iphigenia, commanded by captain Douglas, arrived at Owhyhee in 1788, being the first which touched at that island after the death of captain Cook. There was on board of her a chief of Atooi, named Tianna, who had the preceding year accompanied captain Meares to Canton, and had been enriched by the kindness of his English friends, with a valuable assortment of European articles, arms, and ammunition.

Tianna was a man of great activity and ambition, and a distinguished warrior. These qualities, and his wealth, particularly in fire-arms, rendered him an acquisition of much consequence to an enterprising chief like Tamaahmaah; and he induced him to settle upon Owhyhee, by conferring upon him high rank and extensive tracts of land.

Captain Douglas had with him a small tender, built upon the northwest coast of America. When Tamaahmaah learned this, the idea of having a similar one built, immediately occurred to him; and he pressed that gentleman with so much urgency to allow him the assistance of his carpenter, that he was obliged to give a conditional promise. Although the promise was never fulfilled, Tamaahmaah did not abandon the project; and soon afterwards he prevailed upon an Englishman of the name of Boyd, who had been bred a ship-carpenter, to undertake the construction of a vessel.

About the same time, two other Englishmen, named Young and Davis, of whom some account is given in the work, became resident upon Owhyhee, and with their assistance he determined to build a vessel. Fortunately for the attainment of this object, captain Vancouver arrived, and with the aid of his carpenters, he was enabled to accomplish his favourite object, by the completion of his first decked vessel, the Britannia.

It ought to be mentioned, to his honour, that whilst thus anxious to lay the foundation of a navy, he had in his possession a small schooner, which had been seized by a chief called Tamahmotoo, and which he had carefully preserved, in the hopes of restoring it to her owners.

In 1791 he attacked Titeree, and captured the islands of Mowee, Morotai, and Ranai. Whilst engaged in this expedition, he received information that his own dominions were attacked by Tewarro,* and he was, in consequence, obliged to abandon his conquest and return.

By the energy of his operations he soon vanquished his opponent, who was slain by Tianna, and the whole island of Owhyhee was reduced under his dominion. In the mean time, Titeree, availing himself of his absence, recovered the islands he had lost.

* It is not easy to ascertain the name, or even the identity of this chief, called by captain King Tewarro; by Vancouver, Teamawheere; and by Lisianski, Kiava.

Affairs were in this situation when Vancouver arrived, in March, 1792. He found the islands in a most wretched state, from the long wars that had taken place; and he endeavoured, but without effect, to establish a peace between Titeree and Tamaahmaah.

Tamaahmaah was so sensible of the advantages which would result from a closer connexion with a civilized power, that he made a formal surrender of the sovereignty of the island to the king of Great Britain, with the reservation, that there should be no interference in their religion, internal government, or domestic economy.

Soon after the departure of captain Vancouver, Titeree died, leaving the island of Wahoo to his son Tritoboorie, and Mowee to his son Korkoranee.

A dispute arose between Tritoboorie and his uncle Tahaio, king of Atooi, who laid claim to Wahoo; but Tritoboorie, supported by Mr. Brown, and the crew of the ship Butterworth, not only repelled Tahaio, but even invaded Atooi.

Tamaahmaah, availing himself of these dissensions, invaded and conquered Mowee, Morotai, and Ranai. Next year, 1795, he invaded Wahoo with one detatchment of his force, leaving Tianna to follow him with the other. Whilst waiting the arrival of that chief, he received the unexpected intelligence that he had gone over to the enemy; while, at the same time, an insurrection had broke out in Owhyhee, headed by Nomataha, brother to Tianna. Instead of being overwhelmed by this unexpected intelligence, he took the resolution of instantly attacking his enemies. The war was decided by a sanguinary battle, fought near the village of Whyteete, in which Tamaahmaah was completely victorious.

Young and Davis accompanied him upon this expedition, and were of essential service to him from their knowledge of fire-arms.

Tianna lost his life in the battle, while the sons of Titeree found refuge in Atooi. Tamaahmaah immediately returned to Owhyhee, and soon quelled the insurrection in that island.

He remained there about a twelvemonth ; but either with a view of consolidating the conquests he had already made, or of extending them farther, he proceeded to Laheina, in Mowee, where he resided a few years, and afterwards removed to Wahoo, where he was during the whole time of our author's stay, in 1809 and 1810.

Of the history of Atooi and Onehow, the only islands in the groupe independent of Tamaahmaah, little is known with certainty. Captain King says, that in 1779, they were governed by the grandsons of Perioranne, king of Wahoo. It is probable, that upon the conquest of that island by Titeree, they were also conquered ; for it appears that Tahaio, or Taio, brother of that chief, was king of these islands when captain Vancouver visited them in 1798. He was succeeded by his son Tamoree, or Comaree, who was king of these islands in 1810.

APPENDIX, No. V.

NOTES.

NOTES.

NOTE A.

The author kept a journal in the early part of the voyage; but it was lost in the events which succeeded, and he was afterwards placed in circumstances where it was not in his power to keep one. He has in his possession, however, several documents which serve to ascertain many of the dates. These are,

1st. His letters to his mother, written whenever an opportunity presented itself, and which she preserved.

2d. A certificate from the East-India Company of the time when he quitted their service.

3d. The statement of his case by the Russian surgeon, a translation of which will be found in the Appendix No. II.

The other dates are given from memory, and are either such as a sailor would naturally remember, or circumstances of so remarkable a nature that they could not fail of fixing themselves in a memory much less retentive than that of our author.

Whenever the editor has had it in his power to verify them by collateral authorities, he has not failed to do so; and the result of the inquiry has been, even where corrections were necessary, to show the general accuracy of the narrative: For example, his written account of the first part of the voyage is literally, " The convoy sailed from the Motherbank on 12th May, 1806, and cleared the Channel on the 18th; was twelve weeks on our passage to the Cape of Good Hope; lay at the Cape fourteen or fifteen days; sailed from the Cape about the 19th August, and on the 19th September made the island of St. Paul's; arrived at Pulo Penang about the middle of October, and sailed on the 24th November; left Admiral Trowbridge's flag-ship, the Blenheim; arrived at China the eighteenth January, 1807."

He added, that the convoy left the Cape upon a Friday, and on the three following Saturdays they had each day a gale of wind; that on the third of these Saturdays they passed St. Paul's

Some difficulties arose, however; for, upon consulting the Almanack, the editor found that the 19th August, 1806, was not a Friday, but a Tuesday. Upon asking the reason of his fixing on these particular dates, he showed a letter to his mother, dated Portsmouth, 11th May, saying, the fleet was to sail next day; from whence he concluded the convoy sailed on the 12th; and counting twelve weeks, would fix their arrival at the Cape on Monday, the 4th of August; and fifteen days would make Tuesday, the 19th, as the day they left.

Upon consulting the newspapers of the time, it appears that the fleet did not sail till the 14th of May, and arrived at the Cape on the 7th of August, being just twelve weeks and one day; and fifteen days more fixes the day of sailing on Friday, the 22d. The editor has not discovered whether the other dates in this part of the voyage are correct to a day; but the author says, that the loading of the ships was stopped about six weeks after their arrival, in consequence of the dispute with the Chinese. Counting

Chinese, for whose life this government have required one of the crew to be delivered up, which had been positively refused. This refusal has produced the stoppage of all the chops for that ship ; and Mouqua, (second of the Hong,) by whom she is secured, has been with the linguist for the ship, carried in chains inside of the city. I have conversed with Cheongqua and Conseequa, who have assured me no inconvenience will attend the Americans ; but they assert positively a man must be given up.

"The sailors have behaved most infamously : They hauled down and danced on the Spanish flag, and then destroyed it. Their captain apologized, and next day compelled them to hoist a new one. Some few of the scroundrels showed a disposition to pull down the American colours ; and a part of them were in the act of lowering the Swedish, but were prevented. They have burnt one of the mandarin's houses in front of the factories. This shameful conduct has induced the Chinese to determine, that no more sailors shall be permitted to come up on liberty. It is generally thought the English business, except the country, will all be stopped in a day or two. The English including the Lion man of war, at Bocca Tigris, amount to 1600 men. A few days will decide the unfortunate business."

"*March* 6.—We are every hour afraid of a rupture between the English and Chinese, in consequence of the death of a Chinese, from the accidental stroke of a club by an English sailor.

"The Chinese demanded an Englishman to die, conformable to the laws of their country ; and the English have refused, being unable to find out the person who gave the blow. In consequence, the viceroy of this province gave orders yesterday to stop their trade; and in all probability the next step will be to intercept their supplies, and seize on some person of the factory; a circumstance which must produce the most serious consequences.

"I understand the English have no objection to give up a man, provided they could find out the guilty person; and surely they cannot be blamed for spurning the idea of making an innocent man suffer. God only knows how it will end. They are allowed three days more to decide; and if they do not comply, it is thought the Chinese will endeavour to compel them. Should they be foolish enough to attempt the latter plan, I think they will get a sound drubbing, as the English have now a force at Wampooa and Bocca Tigris of 2000 able-bodied men, all eager for attack."

MORNING CHRONICLE, DECEMBER 4.

Extract of a letter from a gentleman lately resident in China, dated Canton, April 18.

"The affair between the English Company and the Chinese is at length adjusted. After many meetings, chin chinnings, &c. &c. the Chinese government ordered up for trial the fifty-two sailors belonging to the Neptune, that were on liberty when the fray happened. This order was complied with on the part of the Company; and about the 25th of March the sailors arrived in Canton, under the protection of a company of marines from the Lion ship of war. After they had reached Canton, the mandarins intimated that they must be taken into the city for examination. This was resolutely opposed; and it was finally agreed, that the trial should be held in the Company's old factory, the lower part of which was accordingly fitted up in great style, with yellow and crimson silk carpets, cushions, tables, chairs, &c. &c. the whole intended to represent the emperor's court The business now appeared favourable, but was soon shaded by another serious occurrence. The mandarin who was to sit in awful judgment, required that the chief of the Company, the captain of the Lion, and the commodore of the Company's ships, should not be permitted to sit in his presence during the trial. This was not acceded to, and threats were uttered on the part of the British. The mandarin was equally obstinate, and the business assumed a very serious aspect. As the mandarin could not come himself, or send one of high order, he sent one who was willing that the British should sit at their ease in good elbow chairs. Thus arranged, about the 6th instant the trial commenced; and of fifty-two sailors, eleven were selected as the most guilty, and laid over for farther proof. On the 9th, the eleven were again brought up for trial, and two were selected as the guilty persons, who were again laid over for farther investigation. On the 11th, the two were again brought forward, and one of them adjudged guilty, and ordered to be kept in possession of the Company, till the pleasure of the emperor should be known. The British ships are now loading, and will sail in about a fortnight. What fate awaits the sailor retained is uncertain; but it is probable that the mandarins would rather touch a few of the security merchants' dollars, and keep the affair from the emperor, than retaliate the outrage against their countrymen. In this case, not less than one hundred thousand dollars will be necessary to patch up the affair."

In the appendix to Sir George Staunton's account of the Penal Code of China, there is a detailed statement of the proceedings of the Chinese court in this case. The editor has had no opportunity of seeing the work; but the following abstract, taken from the Quarterly Review, Vol. III. p. 315, will show how the cause terminated.

"The British factory was fitted up as a court of justice; the great officers of state, and the judges attended; and the result was, the singling out of eleven men, as having been the most active in the affray. On a re-examination of these men, they endeavoured to prevail on some one to plead guilty, under an implied promise that he should not be punished. This failing, it was suggested that the affair might be got over, if the officers of the Neptune would depose that they had seen a sailor carrying a bamboo stick over his shoulder, against which, in the hurry and confusion, a Chinese had accidentally run his head. The proposal of so ridiculous and pitiful expedient met with the contempt it deserved. The next suggestion was, that some one of the sailors should be prevailed on to state, that finding an attempt made on his pocket, he had struck behind, him, and might thus have wounded the deceased. This expedient meeting with no better success, they proceeded in their examination, and dismissed all except two, Julius Cæsar, and Edward Sheen It appeared that Julius Cæsar had a small cane in his hand on the day of the riot, but was not outside of the factory; and that Edward Sheen was outside of the factory, but did not carry a stick; he confessed, however, that he had a Chinese tobacco pipe in his hand, the tube of which was of bamboo, the court, therefore, decided that he carried a stick, and, consequently, that he was the culprit. Having got thus far over the ground, a long negotiation took place as to the disposal of Edward Sheen, until the final decision of the case should be received from Pekin; and it was at length agreed that he should be left behind in charge of the supercargoes.

" Having thus briefly stated the leading facts, we shall now see in what manner the case was represented to the supreme court at Pekin, and its decision thereupon. It is contained at full length in No. II. of the appendix, p. 521.

" The viceroy of Canton states, for the information of the supreme court, that Edward Sheen, an Englishman, being in the upper story of a warehouse which overlooked the street, and in which there was a window opening with wooden shutters, did, on the 18th day of the first moon, employ a wooden stick, in an oblique direction, to keep open the shutter; and that, in doing this, the wooden stick slipped and fell downwards; that Leao-a-teng, a Chinese, passing at the moment, was struck and wounded by the falling of the said stick upon his left temple, and that on the evening of the following day he died in consequence of the wound. That repeated orders had been given to the chief of the English factory to deliver up the man to justice; that, in reply, it was alleged the said criminal was sick of an ague and fever, and under medical treatment; that on his recovery, he was confronted with the relations of the deceased; that after repeated examinations, the said criminal, Edward Sheen, had acknowledged the truth of all the facts here stated, without reservation; that he had, consequently, been proved guilty of accidental homicide, and ought, therefore, to be sentenced to pay the usual fine, to redeem himself from the punishment of death by strangulation.

"Upon this report the supreme court observes, that the case appears to be one of those acts, of the consequences of which, neither sight, hearing, or reflection, could have given a previous warning; that the said Edward Sheen should, therefore, be allowed to redeem himself from the punishment of death by strangulation, by the payment of a fine (amounting to about 4*l*. 3s. sterling) to the relations of the deceased, to defray the expenses of the burial, and then be dismissed to be governed in an orderly manner in his own country."

It appears that the bribe necessary to procure acquiescence of the parties interested, to this mockery of justice, did not cost the security merchants less than £50,000.

six weeks after the 18th of January, would fix it about the 1st of March. By the accounts from Canton, in Note B, it appears that this actually took place upon the 4th; which renders it probable that the date is correct, or at least pretty nearly so.

In adition to these original documents, the editor has in his possession a number of accounts, in the author's hand, of particular parts of the voyage, and the printed account of his adventures, *in metre*, referred to in the preface.

Immediately after his return, in 1812, a gentleman in Paisley undertook to get an account of his adventures published, provided he drew it up himself. He accordingly made some preparations; but the death of the gentleman prevented the publication.

The Vocabulary was written by the author as he recollected the words, and transmitted to the editor, who arranged them, and afterwards read them over to him, correcting the spelling from his pronunciation, according to the rules which are prefixed to it.

NOTE B, p. 17.

DISPUTE WITH THE CHINESE AT CANTON, IN 1807.

Extract from the Morning Chronicle, 26th August, 1807.

" *Canton, March* 4.—The English Company are involved in considerable trouble, in consequence of some one of the crew of their ship Neptune having killed a

166°
164°
162°
160°
60°
30'
59°
30'
58°
30'
57°
N O R T H
Round I.
70
71
72
74
75
76
77
79
83
88